SCALING SIMPLIFIED!

Unlock the Master Code to Explosive Business Growth by Recruiting a Powerful Team, Attracting Loyal Customers, and Building a Life of Freedom

Shannon Teague

A step-by-step guide to setting the foundations of your business for the Scaling-Up process

Table of Contents

DESIGNING YOUR LIFESTYLE

"Your decisions brought you here, what you do next will regulate your fate – your life is not a pre-determined event; it's something you create with your own bare hands."

– Shannon Teague

Entrepreneurs are undeniably created by their own unique abilities and dreams. People who suddenly harness the prerequisites to enter the ranks of those who want more from life and aren't scared to get out there and take what belongs to them. Seeing people reject their current circumstance and have the audacity to dream; when they do not settle for less and abolish the deepest shell of potential to unlock their maximum capabilities and then improve upon them to achieve the pinnacle of their vision — it's certainly a marvelous sight to behold, isn't it? I am so thrilled to witness that YOU are among those incredible individuals.

This book is what you've been waiting for; it's finally time for you to learn a simplified method of scaling up your profits, have more time in hand and go way beyond your current level to attain your wildest dreams. You may have noticed that this is not just another boring business book that will take you ages to finish; it is on a whole other level. Your perspective about a business book will dramatically change with leaps and bounds – watch out!

When you started your new business, what was in your mind? What were you thinking? What was the life you envisioned for yourself and the people you cherish; after you crossed the shaky bridge that transformed you from a worker to an entrepreneur? Are you living that life? Maybe not yet, but at the end of this book, you will! I can understand how challenging it was for you or anyone to overcome criticism and opinionative comments from knowns and unknowns while starting a business. Yet, you persevered and attained the level you are standing at today.

I can understand that you are struggling to grow your business, improve your finances, and prove people wrong. I know that feeling; I can concede that you need more free time in your business. Currently, you are wearing multiple hats and working for 12-15 hours a day without taking any vacation and still see no visible results. It's tough! Sometimes it also feels that your business owns you and not the other way around. I know the frustration you're going through to scale up your business and finding a simplified step-by-step guide to success. The world is filled with boring books, and it's okay. I am here now to ensure that those things do not fright you anymore – you will soon have the freedom, confidence, and independence you've been looking for in your life.

I may have pushed some buttons here, but it was essential for unlocking that mindset, from which a new version of you will begin to develop. This book is designed to help you scale up your business, be organized to save time, exponentially increase your profits, and create a sustainable business that accommodates your true lifestyle, dream, and financial independence. Even the great Albert Einstein said, "*Any intelligent fool can make things bigger, more complex, and more violent. It takes a touch of genius and a lot of courage to move in the opposite direction.*" I took that quote to heart and started writing a simplified version of business growth strategies for new-age entrepreneurs and business owners like you to help them build the business foundations and start the Scaling Up process– taking a leap into the future in simplifying things for better understanding and clarity; does that make you a genius? Of course!

Nevertheless, you should know what you will be learning in this book, besides the mental attitude and psychology, which incorporates almost 80% of your success. Here is an overview of the nuggets you'll discern in the chapters:

- An easy and simplified explanation for scaling up your business. It will enlighten and inspire you to implement it right away.
- The absolute mindset, required to go to the next level.

- Inherit some impeccable habits of the most successful individuals.
- Unlock your true purpose in life, the art of setting goals and achieving them.
- How to build the company's culture (it's an essential element for growth) and have core values that cannot break under any circumstance.
- How to recruit winners and assemble a powerful team that will take you towards your goals faster.
- How to automate your business so that it can run without you – learn the processes and systems.
- The mystic skill of leadership. Learn how to be a great leader that everyone follows and respects.
- How to simplify your accountings and save more cash in the process.
- How to generate leads interested in your product or services and turn them into raving fans with flawless marketing.
- And so much more...

If the overview gets you excited, hold on until you find unexpected surprises within each chapter – you will thank me later. The principles explained here are not taken from any old business book and are revised. Instead, it is coming from my own experience. I know you may be wondering who I am and how I gained the expertise to write this book? Do you think I will give away my identity just like that? Of course, I will; there is nothing to hide. My name is Shannon Teague. I've been running multiple businesses for eight years, and I've seen all the ups and downs of it. One of my businesses was a recruitment company that deals in the hospitality industry. I couldn't thank the covid-19 pandemic enough for collapsing that baby of mine as it led me on the journey of writing this fantastic book. My goal is to help small businesses like you to establish the success you deserve and dream.

My second start-up was about selling popcorn flavorings to cinemas in the United Kingdom. My business was working in collaboration with giant corporations and blue-collar hotels. I have learned first-hand how difficult scaling up could be and how badly it can affect cash flow in a business if the guidance is inappropriate. It could cause chaos and take the company to its doom. I was hungry for true knowledge and success like you; knowing there is always a higher level to achieve inspired me to learn more. To be the best, you have to learn from the best; I have retained business strategies and growth principles from some of the globe's best business coaches. By combining their wisdom with my years of experience, the massive growth I received was on par with no other. This book is the exact mirror image of my learning curve and the resultant triumph.

My third business is a book publishing company. With my experience, I can systemize everything from the beginning. This strategy solves multiple problems and saves a lot of my time. Since then, I've been using the principles and lessons learned from my experience — they are explained in the book. I am incredibly passionate about starting and growing businesses, reaching financial freedom, taking the profits and reinvesting them into the business and other investment strategies to create generational wealth in many forms. My biggest goal from this publishing business is to teach business owners how to free up their time, travel to the places they love, scale their businesses, and live a successful life.

THE MISTAKES

I was never perfect, and nobody is; I have made mistakes in every element of scaling up. Let me brief you about a few so you can avoid them. One of the biggest mistakes was hiring a team of visionaries. No team member knew how to implement great ideas and keep us on track, including me. I am also a visionary myself. I have many great ideas, but because of that, I don't structure them very well. In scaling up, you must have a team that balances each other's strengths and weaknesses; and a leader that can lead the team while ensuring the systems and goals are followed, and the business is on track. A visionary is equally vital as it provides a clear sense of direction.

My second mistake was offering too many services before the leading service was complete and automated. I also wasn't dedicated to my weekly, quarterly, and yearly goals. Did you know that having a well-mechanized system in place adds very minimal stress to the business? I learned it the hard way. When a member exits and removes the owner from the business, it doesn't crumble; instead, it runs smoothly without them. Look at McDonald's; anybody could join up and flip burgers. The system is so powerful that it sustains anyone. They will train people and get them to work.

My third mistake was not being financially ready to scale up my business and increase profits. I lost a lot of money before I learned that having a CFO can ensure healthy cash flow, money lending responsibilities, and an accurate cash distribution plan; hence enforcing growth. Managing and leading your team is also paramount because hiring a team enables new issues in your business. You'll feel like you're constantly solving problems and getting nowhere. In order to save time, effective systems should be in place so that each role is carried out successfully. You can witness visible effects in the marketing department. Formulate solid marketing strategies for your product/services and remember that everything in your business must be tracked and measured using KPIs; ensuring that every staff member performs to their highest level – even YOU!

I've also been running my business remotely for more than six years. I structured them in a specific way that enabled me to travel and live anywhere globally, all while my business was making me more affluent in the UK. Although I mostly live in SE Asia because rent and living expenses are comparatively cheaper here. It qualifies me to spend less, live a better lifestyle, and reinvest all the profits into my business for more growth. I want to show you how you can also live wherever you want using the book's principles to design your life. My book is the clue you've been waiting for, don't live a meaningless story.

I am an expert in this topic because I've failed, learned, and improved myself to gain success. You know what they say about failure and experience, don't you? It is the best teacher! I want to educate you, and I am ready to walk you through the entire process. Are you ready to walk by my side, learn all the lessons, and implement them? Whoa!!! Slow down, that was a loud 'YES.' I guess you are excited now, aren't you? I've set a high standard for this book, and it's now time to meet every one of them. So, let's climb the pinnacle and wave down at your competitors. It will be fun! Up we go!

A contrasting Image to signify what people think success looks like v/s what it actually is!

CHAPTER ONE

MINDSET FOR SUCCESS

"You have power over your mind - not outside events. Realize this,
and you will find strength."

— Marcus Aurelius

Humankind has been blessed with the gift of mind that no other creature possesses; it makes us stand on top of the food chain. But, what else do you think your mind is capable of? Everything! This chapter will set your negative notions on fire and provide you with a growth mindset. You will soon discover that this mindset is an asset, especially for the success of your business. It has been proven countless times that triumph or defeat in any area of your life results from your mindset. Recall your achievements, such as starting a company, hiring your first employee, landing your first project, and your first customer; every one of those accomplishments is the result of having a "nailed it" attitude!

Most people believe that having a successful mindset is the easy part; this enables them to move ahead and interface with their businesses. However, they fail to realize that success is an imbalanced relationship between business and mindset. Those who amalgamate their business affairs with an appropriate mindset; experience exponential growth in every segment of life. It's not something you do once at the beginning of your business and then push aside later on; it is a continuous cycle that needs to work in conjunction with each other. The reason I referred to success as an imbalance relationship is that the mindset is paramount. However, the ratio differs with a huge gap. To gain success, you could easily say that you need 25-30 percent business skills (that includes communication, ideas, procedures, execution, structures, etc.), and the remaining 75-80 percent comes from your mindset.

I could see those jaws drop on the floor; I'll wait while you pick them back up. No successful person will deny the fact mentioned above because they know how difficult it was for them to build that mindset in the first place. I could provide you with an excellent team, significant cash flow, and abundant resources, but if you don't have the right mindset, I am afraid that all those favors will go in vain. So, relinquish a negative mindset and step outside of your comfort zone; it's the only way to grow. It doesn't matter who you are, where you came from, your background, or anything else – what matters is how you think!

Your actions are equal to the view you have for yourself, your business, customers, and employees. The body follows the mind. Your job is to harness the energy within yourself and transform your body into a powerful tool that works in harmony with the greatest asset of all — your mind. The day you can accomplish this, you will find yourself closer to your dreams. Don't forget me when you achieve success; you're welcome!

Life coach Elyse Santilli said, *"It's a daily decision to dig deep into your soul, align with the human you were born to be, and do the things you're called to do."* Of course, your calling is your business, and what you envisioned yourself doing, the success you crave for will come from your calling. Firstly, however, it is paramount to ask yourself who you need to be to deserve that title of greatness. The only reason you do not have your name on the wall of fame is that the person who truly deserves that title is yet to be discovered. Therefore, I want you to do yourself a favor — take the liberty of accepting who you are at any given level and leverage that understanding to upgrade your features, skills, habits, and perspective.

The life you desire is on the other side of that mountain. However, you should decide whether to climb the mountain, face your fears and step out of your comfort zone to reach the success you crave, or to stay at the bottom of the mountain where it is comfortable, familiar, and no growth is achieved. I understand it well because I was hungry for success and had to advance on a perpetual self-discovery mission to realize that my mindset was stopping me from climbing that huge mountain. Eventually, I discovered that standing at the bottom of the mountain is more uncomfortable because my fears prevented me from reaching my potential and finding my authentic self.

YOU ARE ENOUGH

You may not be used to this phrase, but I believe it to be true: **you are destined for greatness**. You are a miracle and blessing on your own. There were trillions of others waiting to be born, but you took the plunge, and here you are, there are more than 7 billion people in this world. You chose to become an entrepreneur in the business of helping other people elevate their lives. But, most importantly, you got your hands on this book designed to enhance you and your business – your existence matters. You are the lightning bolt striving towards success, and no matter what happens, you will not stop at anything but the number one spot. *"Success is the sum of small efforts, repeated day-in, and day-out."* – Robert Collier.

Nelson Mandela was a force to be reckoned with; he changed the course of the world by fighting against racism and became the first ever South African President in 1994 through a democratic voting system. He won by 62%. Before his five-year presidency, he was an activist who fought the "apartheid" movement and came out victorious. To say that his life was difficult would be an understatement. He was prisoned and tormented, but his oath to protect his people allowed him to persevere. He built a mindset, the likes of which was never seen before; he wasn't the most powerful nor most influential person, and had no political support; he started by himself, and people noticed that a wave of change had risen. In his life, he won more than 250 awards, among which was a Nobel Peace Prize.

He could have given up millions of times when facing challenges, nobody would have blamed him, and he would still be renowned as someone who tried to liberate the South Africans, but that wasn't his goal. He was ready to take on any challenge until he achieved the outcome he envisioned. His mindset changed history; imagine what you are capable of achieving if you change your mindset?

You, too, can harness the power within and make this world a better place to live. There will probably be obstacles, setbacks, and failures along the way, but you cannot take these obstacles as permanent defeat. Get over the thought of failure and begin the journey for GREATNESS because you are not an ordinary person - you are the chosen one.

FOCUS ON CHANGE

You are probably wondering: if you are enough and a miracle on its own, then why haven't you discovered your greatness yet? That's a valid question, and this section will provide you with an answer. Most people in the world live in one of the three following states:

- **State 1**: Below potential: This is the state where people are living below their means; they haven't discovered their ultimate potential yet. The majority of society lives here.
- **State 2**: Living their potential: This is where they realize what they're capable of and do just that. These people are doing what they love and on a level that is above most people.
- **State 3**: Absolute potential: These people are bored to live within their potential and aim to constantly outgrow themselves. They want more juice out of life, and they refuse to stay within their limits.

It doesn't matter which state you begin with, state one or state two, but your ultimate goal should be to reach state three, which is where you will feel fulfillment, happiness, and abundance. Money is not the final goal, you will surely be wealthy, but your primary goal should always be, living your passion, providing massive value, and helping people. *"The mind becomes rich before the pockets get full"* - Sheldon the Sniper. To do that, you need to develop yourself. What got you here won't take you to the next level. You need to change and analyze yourself; discern the habits inhibiting you from exploring your capabilities. Allow me to provide you with quick tips that could be implied immediately and replace your daily routine with a successful version.

- **Sleep like a baby**: You need to sleep well. I know that you're stressed with your business and its growth, but if that keeps you up all night, it's not worth it. You won't be super productive the next day, and don't count on your decisions to bear fruit. *So, sleep well today and know that everything is going to be alright tomorrow.*

- **Meditation and breathing**: In today's world, this technique is a master tool to keep your mind focused and ease anxiety which most business owners will experience on an ongoing basis. Connecting with your body and mind by sitting still and breathing uniformly will help you understand yourself better and allow you to have more control over your thoughts and emotions. You can then segregate your limiting beliefs and work on them to improve the overall quality of your life.

- **Have an inspiring vision**: Goals need attention. For example, you will have a dream of what you want to accomplish in your business. Make sure that the goal is more than money and benefits more people than you and your team. It is imperative to set time aside (probably after a meditation session) to visualize yourself in those dreams so that you trick your mind into finding ways to achieve them.

- **Practice affirmation**: It is the art of fostering your beliefs, empowering positive thinking, and enhancing self-empowerment. Practicing affirmation must be your daily habit alongside meditation and envisioning, so that you can teach your brain to believe the language you tell yourself. Then, repeat it enough times so that your brain finds creative ways to achieve your goals.

- **Exercise**: Nobody is interested in becoming the most successful person in the graveyard. You need to be physically fit to take on challenges, which is why you should exercise at least three times a week for 30-60 minutes. Exercising will keep you healthy, productive, feeling fresh, and help you overcome mood swings.

- **Read books**: Especially mine! It is a great way to train your mind to learn and expand its horizon. For example, you can read multiple books on personal development and business, and autobiographies, or anything that inspires and motivates you to achieve your goals.

- **Practice gratitude**: The more grateful you are, the more you will have. Shit happens to all of us, which might shift your thoughts to negative thinking, but prevent yourself from going down a negative spiral, wake up early and write down five things that you are grateful for in your life and see the difference – you will thank me later with a present (by the way, I like flowers).

- **Be productive**: You may feel that this is obvious, but it is not. Most business owners spend their time on things that occupy the majority of their day and not a single second in productivity. For example, spending 10 hours in your office means nothing if all you do is sign some documents and attend a few meetings. Being productive means doing the actual work taking you and your business towards the dream and goal you envisioned – think again. Consistency is key to reaching success.

To get far in life and reach your potential, you need to keep pushing yourself regardless of what life throws at you. We all suffer disgrace and humiliation from time to time, we all experience family problems and suffer grief and regret, but it doesn't mean that we should throw in the towel and sulk. *Life laughs at the people who give up. You are not among them and will never be.* You will never give your haters the option or the satisfaction to laugh at you and see you back down.

You may be down, you may be out cold, you may have received the biggest knock-out punch ever, but that is still not an excuse for you to stay down. You must stand up, dust off all the dirt, and smile because you are ready for round 2! Bring it on. Being an underdog may sound cool, but it comes with its fair share of struggles and hard work. This phrase reminds me of the Rocky movie. I recall round-14 of Rocky one. It was the fight between a beginner named Rocky and the best boxer in the world, Apollo Creed. It was difficult to see Creed beating up Rocky and throwing him from one side of the ring to another. He was getting smacked, jabbed, and every other boxing trick played at him. He kept getting up. For most people, it makes no sense why he kept standing. Creed kept killing Rocky, and everybody in the audience told him to stay down, even his coach. Finally, Creed knocked him down and thought that he got Rocky, now victory was his, and he accepted it by turning around and raising his hands in the air.

Rocky found strength somewhere within him, took the ring's support, and started to climb back up. When Creed turned towards Rocky, his face seemed as if his soul had left his body. He was shocked to see him on his feet again. I am sure he must have questioned who this guy was and where he came from, and that's the end of the story. I want you to have a rock-solid never give up attitude. Regardless of how many punches you have taken from life, you promise me that you will shake it off and stand back up until victory is yours.

PERSPECTIVE IS EVERYTHING

Difficult roads often lead to beautiful destinations, and I want this road to end with you living your ultimate dream. Your perception means everything to you. Everyone has a different perspective on life. We all hold different things dear to us. Some people care more about money, and some care more about relationships. The problems you have in your life are the result of your decision and perspective. To solve them, all you have to do is look at them from a different perspective. *Don't look at your business as a never-ending challenge that you can't seem to overcome. Instead, look at it as a mountain you want to climb to reach the top.*

Perspective means the way you look at something. For example, two people could look at the same number from the opposite side. One might say it's a 6, while the other might argue that it's a 9. It's tiring and develops fear within you. The minute you identify a problematic situation, you might panic and make a rash decision that may drown you even further. Still, when you take time off, breathe, and look at it from a different view, suddenly everything makes sense. You see a way out, and not just that, you also spot opportunities for you and the people around you. Use the great power of perspective to defeat your worries, fears, and problems. Do not feel insecure and take unwanted actions because there is a chance that it might backfire. Business is a game where a series of right or wrong decisions could either make you a fortune or cost you one – the choice is yours. One wrong or right move will not change your entire history, but the day will come when you fail to learn from your mistakes. "*Don't be trapped by dogma — which is living with the results of other people's thinking.*" – Steve Jobs.

Sometimes, the problem that is eating you up isn't the actual problem; your perspective is. You may have been looking at things with the wrong perspective, and the problem vanishes when you turn it around. It is a powerful question to ask yourself. Setbacks may appear, but the only time you fail is when you give up. Never stop until you reach your end goals. "*Your perspective is always limited by how much you know. Expand your knowledge, and you will transform your mind.*" – Bruce H. Lipton.

If you started your business solely to make money, it could be one of the ceilings limiting you from breaking the shackles. Instead, understand what your clients are looking for and be their solution. You exist on the face of the earth to provide value and make people's lives easier. The sooner you understand this, the faster your business will grow. It's just a simple shift from money to value, but it dramatically changes the entire outcome — money will evidently be the by-product. With passion comes success.

We have 100% complete control over our perceptions. For example, the pandemic has caused damage to millions of people around the world. You and I cannot change the circumstances of the pandemic, but we can control how we react to them. You can either be sad, angry, feel lonely because you are away from your dear ones, or you could perceive it as an opportunity to discern investments that will provide extraordinary returns in the upcoming years, get in tune with yourself, and transform your business to work remotely. Perception will allow you to break those chains and make better decisions for yourself – ponder on it.

CONTROL YOUR EMOTIONS

Shifting perception is only impactful when you keep your emotions in check and do things beneficial to you. I am telling you this because we quickly react to any problem or unforeseen circumstances and end up hurting ourselves. Don't panic when things aren't going your way. Doing something you will regret later isn't worth a dime. An old Chinese proverb reads, "*control your emotions, or they will control you.*"

Most people let their feelings and emotions to overpower them, and that decision has consequences. I am not telling you that you should be a stone-hearted person. I mean, who wants that? But you should know when to react to your thoughts and when to swallow them to do what is suitable for everyone.

- **Step 1**: Train your mind to be calm in every situation. Your mind is capable of amazing things, but it doesn't make rational decisions while sitting alongside your emotions. It only takes a few seconds for your brain to activate the fight or flight defense mechanism. When you're fuelled with rage, you act quickly and regret your reaction once the anger subsides. Step one is to be aware of where that feeling comes from, meaning the situation that triggered it and its reason.

- **Step 2:** Understand your true anger level, which means understanding the intensity of the emotion; how hurtful it is for you? Make yourself aware about it.

- **Step 3:** Master the breathing technique. Practice a breathing technique when you are filled with anger; your rage will slowly lose all control over you. The power will be back within your grasp.

- **Step 4:** Practice realization. Let me give you a simple tool that will help you to regain consciousness and think straight. It's called **"the realization."** As soon as you detect that you're starting to lose control over your power, close your eyes and realize that you have a secret tangible crystal that shines like a real diamond. During this emotional chaos, you are handing it out to the person who caused the anger. Are you willingly going to give away your precious crystal? I didn't think so. Take deep breaths and pull your hand back. The other person doesn't deserve that crystal as much as you do. The only way to stop that from happening is to *realize* that your actions are more precious than a quick burnout - calm yourself down by breathing and don't be reactive within those first few moments of anger.

When you are swallowed within your emotions, you do not see things clearly. It clouds your judgment and surfaces new options that either hurt you, your business, or people around you. If you have a sudden rush of emotions during any situation, ask yourself these five questions:

1. What am I not seeing in this situation?
2. Is getting furious and snapping at everybody a really good way to react? And more importantly, how will I feel after my anger has subsided and I lose control of my emotions?
3. Does being upset and exasperated open doors to new options?
4. What action can I take today to deal with this problem forever?
5. Are there more ways in which I could overcome this obstacle?

Do you remember the importance of perspective that we discussed earlier? Well, use it here! We can't control how we feel; however, we can control our reactions. We all have triggers from childhood, past experiences, etc. We all have a right to feel the way we do, and I believe that the only way to overcome the trigger is by understanding it and allowing space for the feeling to pass. The more we understand our emotions, triggers, and feelings, the more power we have over our reactions.

These questions will help you calm yourself down and present a roadmap to finding solutions and making decisions that favor everyone. *"Life is not about finding yourself. Life is about creating yourself."* – Lolly Daskal. Create a version that does not react quickly – control your mind; control your emotions.

EXPLORING OPPORTUNITIES

Your mindset should be your most powerful ally. Think of every problem as an opportunity to learn a crucial lesson. Excitement should arise when unforeseen situations appear because it is an opportunity for growth within yourself and your business. A few losses aren't something to cry about, instead, learn and be grateful for the lessons because the same problem is unlikely to occur again if the lesson has been discovered. *Forget the loss; remember the lesson.*

Have a glass half full mentality because being negative never worked out for anyone. Success goes hand in hand with positivity. You will never find any successful person with a negative mindset, why do you sit thinking that something terrible will happen? I know business is unpredictable, but predicting failures isn't helping either. Instead, our mind will unconsciously lead us to this path, as that is the message we are telling ourselves daily. Remember, our body goes where our mind walks. Make a choice not to be emotional and scared. Once you reach this level of control over your mind, you will see opportunities rather than obstacles.

There is good in every situation if we are open to seeing it, but we are so fixated on looking at the negative that we close our eyes to the gifts presented to us through the "negative" experiences. As I like to say, *"with every negative experience comes a natural positive outcome; it is the polarity of life."*

I like to believe that every problem I am going through is only being presented to make me stronger. There is a huge reward waiting for me at the finish line, and to be worthy of the success I desire and to shine like a diamond, I need to persevere through the pressure – a healthy mentality, isn't it? If I hadn't experienced any negativity or push back or, most importantly, didn't choose to see the lesson; I wouldn't be where I am today in my life and my business. So be open to the lesson; until then, life will keep presenting the same situations until you have learned it. Have you ever wondered why the same thing keeps happening to you? Why do you keep dating the same kind of person? Why do the same mistakes keep happening in your life and business? Maybe try changing your outlook next time to see what you can learn from your experience; that will empower you to grow and move forward not to face this situation again.

Don't complain about having problems; try embracing them. Every fear and doubt can be turned into an incredible opportunity if you open your mind to lessons and growth. J.K. Rowling was rejected 12 times; she went ahead and self-published anyway – the rest is history. Thomas Edison is said to have failed 10,000 times before discovering the light bulb. Just imagine if he would've stopped after the 20th attempt, would we still have the discovery? Maybe, or maybe not, the lesson here is never to give up no matter how many times you suffer failure. You can't know how to run a business successfully unless you have actually run one and made many mistakes to learn from along the way. There is no straight line to success. We need these healthy lessons and mistakes along the way to become more successful, run a better business, understand our weaknesses, and improve ourselves.

Let me tell you about a situation we faced a while ago in one of my businesses. We once dealt with a hotel that did not pay our invoices for six months. It was for the shifts that our team attended. We chased the client every day; he was a spa manager.

Eventually, after days of reminding and threatening to take legal action, the client gave in. He connected us directly to the hotel's finance team, where we spoke with the director, who signed off all the payments. We surprisingly discovered that our invoices never reached his desk; this caused severe stress because we were supposed to pay our team every week for the shifts, they attended regardless of whether we received the payment or not.

As a small business, the payment was detrimental to our cash flow. However, after communicating with the finance director and threatening to take legal action, our invoice was paid immediately. Nevertheless, we learned from experience and revised our terms and conditions, amending an additional fine for late payments. Furthermore, we also created a branded T&C that highlighted all our payment-related terms to be easy to read, only because our original T&C entailed all of our company's terms - it was a lot of information to consume. The branded T&C was a simple printable document that could be kept on the desk for quick access.

In addition, the T&C became a critical part of the payment system, helping us understand who the person responsible for processing payments was and requested their contact details when signing new contracts. From that day forward, before signing a new contract, we always contacted the finance director and the manager via email, clearing out the payment queries so that both parties can understand the usage of our services.

We also installed a follow-up and reminder system that enabled our finance team to notify the client and their finance department about the due payments a week prior. The message included the scheduled payment date, payable amount, and the applicable late fees if the transaction wasn't processed in the given time. We also sent a notification one day before the due payment. Despite that, we sent a third reminder with our payment policies, illustrating late fees if we didn't receive the payment on time. We paid particular attention to keeping the messages clear and friendly.

After implementing the reminder system in the business, we hardly experienced any late payments, and it helped us keep our cash flow consistent.

THE BELIEF SYSTEM HOLDING YOU BACK

As children, we are programmed to have a belief system about ourselves by our parents, teachers, or surroundings. I challenge you to question those installed beliefs and evaluate whether they are limiting or strengthening you? If the prior is true, shatter those beliefs and adopt a new version that supports your mission, helps you discover your potential, and takes you closer to success. As kids, we could not differentiate good from bad, but now we are well-equipped to know the difference. There is no reason you should still hold on to any unhealthy beliefs about money, rich people, methods of making money, business ethics, and whatever other beliefs limiting your growth.

The world may entice you to remain the same and keep your identity as who you are, but if you do not transform into the best version of yourself, chances are there will be no fulfillment in your life. You will make the same amount of money, work the same hours, meet the same people, and live in the same city. Is it worth investing in a predictable, constant future? BAD IDEA! In my experience and that of many people I know, we usually aren't given the foundations as children to fully develop into the adults we envision ourselves to be. Instead, we are constantly fed information and taught destructive behaviors by external sources that don't align with the adult we imagine, the improved version of ourselves. These beliefs remain intact, and as the year's pass, it becomes difficult to eliminate them.

You must have heard the phrase "be yourself," but who is that? Who do you want to be? If you aren't clear who you want to be, how will you ever become yourself? And even if you know who you are, do you want to be that version of yourself? Or would you rather be a better and improved version? I learned negative behaviors as a child, which were used as a protective mechanism. One of which was to raise my voice high when expressing my feelings.

It was the communication method used in my home growing up. As I got older and more self-aware, it became clear that I was not too fond of this characteristic in myself, to say the very least. Therefore, I went on a self-discovery mission to change the behaviors that didn't align with the person I wanted to be through many months of therapy, meditation, journaling, and practicing affirmations to change the language I use to communicate to my brain. I soon discovered through hard work that I can change every aspect of myself that does not align with the person I want to be. Please don't mistake me; this isn't an easy journey at all, but as the saying goes, "nothing worth having comes easy." It takes hard work and determination to design the life we want and be the person we envision.

If you have the life you desire, then you have done the work and have developed yourself enough to be fulfilled in your life. But if you envision your life to be different and dream about a better, more exciting, and fulfilled life, you need to start forming new habits and changing the behaviors that don't align with this dream. I've seen people walk the path, working hard, and chasing their dreams, but suddenly they lose momentum, and their old beliefs kick in, fear is formed, and they never cross the finish line. I don't think you want to be among those who could see the finish line but never crossed it? Self-development is a never-ending journey.

This is your identity, remove the limits that other people have placed upon you and go all out. Dream big and back those dreams with extraordinary efforts and dedication. Affirm to yourself that you are meant to achieve great things, get down from the hamster wheel, and show the world your mystic powers to get what you say you want.

QUICK TASK

Your belief system is built from various events, knowledge, experience, environment, visualization, advice, etc., and you need to understand each of those beliefs. So, I have created a small task for you to be acquainted with those beliefs and, more importantly, overcome them. First, be honest with yourself and write ten belief systems you were taught in your life that you think could be holding you back. Now that you have a long list, it's time to shatter those beliefs by replacing them with a positive belief system. Follow the steps below to start your journey:

- **Affirm daily**: This is a powerful tool that will help you to overcome your limiting beliefs. For instance, if you have a belief about money and wealth, you could recite affirmations about it and how it can be used to create value and help other people.

- **Focus on your purpose**: Understand why you are doing the things you are committed to, have a strong reason for every goal, and remind yourself of the reason. For instance, if you've seen the horrors of poverty, this could be the biggest motivator for you to become wealthy. Never forget your purpose in life.

- **Have a success journal**: It is always good to keep your eyes on the prize, but it is also important to pat your back and count your successes. So have a journal where you can highlight all your past and future achievements and lessons. It will remind you that you are doing great in life and help you keep track of your progress when you face difficult situations, lose your motivation, or are drowning in a negative mindset; this remarkable tool will prompt you of your amazing achievements.

- **Establish the smallest task**: You know what you want in life, but getting started is the hardest part. Therefore, it is suggested to decide on the smallest yet most important task you could execute right now that will take you towards your wildest dreams. Then, get into the habit of starting your day with the top priority tasks.

I hope this chapter has shattered your limiting beliefs and provided you with the appropriate mindset for success. You next move towards success is building positive habits that work in conjunction with your mindset. So, let's move ahead and learn about healthy habits in the next chapter. See you there...

CHAPTER TWO

GREAT HABITS

"Depending on what they are, our habits will either make us or break us. We become what we repeatedly do."

— Sean Covey

Repetition is the pillar upon which the foundation of success or failure stands. What you do repeatedly is who you become. I call them habits. If you eat eight times a day, spend six hours watching TV, and skip a workout, who do you think you will become? A painful picture, isn't it? To become the best version of yourself, you need certain habits that will support you. Nobody wishes to get fat, unproductive or lazy; it is the result of your habits. In business, having positive habits is essential to determine your future. You won't just become successful; you need to be disciplined and create good habits. Just because you came here to learn about business growth doesn't mean that you as an individual have nothing to do with it; your personal and your professional habits are responsible for your successful reign.

Richard Branson has the same amount of time as you, so why does he have billions? You may be thinking that he and all the other entrepreneurs who hit the jackpot are built differently. That is partially true. It is the fact that they are different from ordinary people, but what sets them apart is their willingness to conquer their thoughts, embrace their flaws, and thrive with impeccable disciplinary habits. Without their habits, there is no way he or anybody else has got any chance of being the richest man in the whole world.

BENEFIT OF HABITS

Your business is in the initial years, isn't it? Well, are you aware of the habits that are holding you back? If not, then let this chapter be the driving force for that change within you. Great men and women aren't born great; they **attract greatness** by implying the code that depicts the ultimate difference – habits. When you witness success, the first question that you and most people ask is, *"how did you become successful?"* The question stands correct, but their assumptions are wrong. You are looking for a shortcut, cheatsheet, or any other way in which you could impersonate their wealth in the quickest time frame. However, you should instead look for the habits they bestowed upon themselves, the hardships they endured, and all the failures committed along the way. These things will give you way more clarity than any cheatsheet ever could.

There is a small percentage of people in this world who set a goal and achieved it. For instance: losing 50Kgs within 12 months, reading 50 books every year, earning their first $100k, and many more. But when most people set a goal, they reach nowhere near the halfway mark and quit. Why is that? Because they lack the required discipline that comes through owning productive habits. One way or another, we all have certain habits; there are specific things we do every day or periodically, and there is just no getting rid of them. The question here is, are these habits taking you closer to your ultimate goal or away? Because if the latter is true, then is it wise to hold on to those habits? Let that sink in... I would have tossed them right out of my life like a ball, and I did. I was overwhelmed with the negative habits that were getting in the way of my business. It was hard, but I eventually learned to stay without them. I even replaced them with other fun, engaging, and productive habits. Trust me; you could develop the grit too!

Whether your goal is to grow your business substantially, get more free time to focus on the more important stuff, or live a life of abundance, the simple key to having it all is habits. Make sure that you are practicing certain activities regularly; it acts as a prerequisite towards business growth—ever wondered how certain things come naturally to some people and why you couldn't even come close? Well, it is the result of consistent action over a period of time. Bruce Lee said, "*I fear not the man who has practiced 10,000 kicks once, but I fear the man who has practiced one kick 10,000 times.*" That's just it. When you learn to harness healthy habits, things will come naturally to you; you will be more effective and efficient with the outcome.

Your business must signify who you are as a person, and when you finally develop those habits, you come face to face with the real you. Finding yourself is the biggest reward a person could ever earn. In the social media world, where most people are wearing a mask to gain exposure, being who you really are, a unique personality that enriches every soul, is a blessing in disguise.

Take any successful person you know; they first needed to find themselves before stumbling upon the strategy to grow their businesses. Ask them how they did it and model their way to find your unique version; they will tell you that even during the tough times when sales were down, when people were abandoning them, when the market was brutal, they still showed up every day. They didn't fall into the trap of the devil that approaches in the form of failures.

Instead, they were intelligent about the path that would lead them to fairies and angels – they found it, and through sheer perseverance and persistence, which worked as their tools through consistent implementation. They didn't waste time waiting for something to motivate them; they got inspired themselves through consistency and faith that tomorrow will be far better than today – isn't that the mere definition of habit? Of course, it is.

If you want people to look up to you and follow you as a true leader in a business environment, you need to set an example through your actions. Your habits hold the power of projecting your image onto others. They do what they see, and when your employees see you working twice as hard, they will push their limits to join your league. I heard it in an interview when an employee from Tesla testified the following phrases, "*it is hard not to put in 80 hours a week when you look at Elon Musk putting in a 100 or more.*" Musk has set an example for his people not to perceive him as a boss, but as someone they work with and look up to for inspiration. They follow in his footsteps and try to match his class. Leading by example is how communities are built and how cultures are formed.

People have elders in the community who follow a path that is righteous and rewarding according to them. They practice certain habits and inspire people from several generations to follow the same. The key foundation of all is still habits. Benjamin Franklin explained that "*your net worth to the world is usually determined by what remains after your bad habits are subtracted from your good ones.*"

Let me ask you this right now, what is your net worth? Calm down, no need to panic, it was a point-blank question, but you still have the time to formulate an answer from your own life. If there is any form of ambiguity, then increment some positive habits and scrutinize the outcome one more time to answer the question.

Habits are an exciting form of activity that holds the power to change your overall life. Of course, the majority of the people who believe in the power of habits affirm the statement that "one habit improves one phase of life," however, only a few people are aware of the truth that there are habits that not only improves a single phase of life but with time, increases the overall quality of your life as well. I've witnessed it when I was implementing a habit of managing my thoughts by staying calm and collected to make better business decisions. Still, it turns out that this habit also reduces my stress amid facing chaos in my personal life. It also enables me to have a second perspective towards any situation that assists me in finding appropriate solutions and opens a new world of opportunities and qualitative approaches.

"You'll never change your life until you change something you do daily. The secret of your success is found in your daily routine." – John Maxwell. Let me give you another example: committing to exercise is a way to look good and feel confident, but it also intensifies productivity, management of time and energy, and improves your mental health. It's game time pals, how many habits could you think of at the top of your head that falls under this category? Go ahead, list them all down. The one

with the longest list wins. While you're at it, install it into your life as well – that's your prize!

HABITS OF SUCCESSFUL PEOPLE

When we talk about habits, it's only fair to provide you with a few habits that most successful people practice daily. Then, match your own life with these habits, and let's see how many you already have and how many are pending. Shall we?

1. **Journaling**: This is a great way to reduce stress, learn more about any situation you may be facing, have a better understanding of who you are, formulate a different perspective, plan your life, and overall have a significant qualitative life. Successful people use journals to set goals and keep track of their progress, gratitude, track their habits, remind themselves about important stuff, and release the thoughts clogging their minds. So, start writing today!

2. **Exercise:** Becoming successful is only complete when you have a healthy body to experience all the fun. As Tony Robbins said, "*you do not want to be the richest man in the graveyard.*" Workout every day for 30-60 minutes minimum, and you will feel the energy within.

3. **Disposing negativity**: Many successful people avoid negative influences like social media disputes, Twitter, news, unsolicited emails, and more. Keep negativity

away from you so that you can only attract positivity towards you like a magnet.

4. **Learn daily**: There is no excuse for why you couldn't read two pages from a business book every day. You should never lose your learning curve. Learn about your industry, master your concepts, ostracize the outdated versions and elevate the latest technology to enhance your business.

5. **Network**: your network is your net worth, and the more connected you are to your network, the better it is for you. Be wary of the people you include here because you are looking to be the best; it is suggested that you keep people of a different scale, learn from them, and implement the lessons.

However, one of the critical habits you could develop today is the habit of actually getting things done. Regardless of your knowledge, the reward will be exponential to the person who gets things done. Are you a doer? That's the roar; I love it! Now, how do you become a great doer? That's a compounding effect. When you commit to something every day, eventually, you become a master in it because now you've turned that daily task into a habit. When you make an effort to wake up at 5 am every day for the next 30 days, there will come a time when you wouldn't even need an alarm clock. Your body will respond to the surroundings, and your eyes will open. If you are ever scared of what the future holds for you, do not fright, look at your habits today, and based on that, you could assume your future.

HOW TO CREATE HABITS?

It is excellent to self-reflect and understand a little more about your current self and where to place certain habits. Get the balance, and you will gain the advantage. Habits prevent you from spending additional energy on things. Our mind is looking to create patterns as it needs to save energy as much as possible. Therefore, all you have to do is repeat the process enough times so that your mind picks it up and registers it as a habit. Do you need to focus before walking? NO! Walking every day is a habit; you get the gist, don't you?

Charles Duhigg, the author of *"the power of habit,"* teaches a simple method to evaluate and create habits. He explains that every habit integrates three crucial steps: cue, routine, and reward. Cue is the trigger that allows your mind to initiate autopilot and execute the registered habit. A routine is a mental, physical, or emotional regime you follow to reach your outcome. reward is the outcome you gain after executing the routine. Your brain determines the value of your habit based on your reward factor. For example, if you have a habit of fastening your seat belt as soon as you enter the car, that's a good habit, with the reward being safety and security. Here, your cue could be opening the car door; routine could be stepping in with the right foot first, followed by the left one, and then fastening the seat belt. You get the picture. *"Good habits are worth being fanatical about."* – John Irving.

Using this theory, you could create new habits for yourself. Find a habit you want to develop, create a cue that will trigger your process, set a routine that you follow every day, and then proffer yourself with an appropriate reward for carrying out that task. When you repeat this process daily, it will turn into a habit; voila!

You can play around with this technique, change the cue, reward, or even the routine if you want to get the change, but the important thing is still sticking to it consistently for over a month. The more appealing your reward is, the more interesting the routine is, the quicker you could assign a cue to it and bring it into your life.

There is something I need to tell you before it's too late. Learn to manage your energy using your willpower. The goal is to save energy and utilize it on things that matter. We humans only have a set amount of energy to spare every day, so figuring out where your energy should flow becomes very important to you and me. Of course, it's necessary to use it for exercise, but do not waste it on mundane tasks like emails.

Here is a small task for you: create a morning and evening routine. Set a particular time for waking up and going to bed. Next, you need to create a routine to follow as you wake up and are about to go to sleep. Exercise is a great way to start the day, and meditation to end the day.

DEFAULT DIARY

To create significant habits in your business, we will be using a system called default diary. It means having a regular recurring block of time covering different aspects of your business. It avoids piling up tasks and reduces stress. For example, your first day of the week can be dedicated to business development tasks. After that, you might come up with multiple developmental ideas throughout the week. However, at this point, you've already allocated a time slot to brainstorm, and for that reason, you don't have to drop your current task. Just write the idea down and leave it until the time comes. Furthermore, you can also allocate a day for marketing. Create manageable tasks and focus on them individually. Biweekly, you can spend a couple of hours on your financial matters. For some reason, if invoicing is slipping away from your to-do list, this is the time to focus and get it done.

The idea and purpose of the default diary are to take your quarterly goals and dedicate time each day and week to attain these goals. You should be dedicating time to working on your business, not in your business. Leave time for unforeseen tasks that pop up in the day and manage these tasks (that take all your time but don't gear you toward your goals) in those allocated times only. The idea is to focus on one task at a time and forget about others. Nobody became super productive by taking on ten tasks at once. When you allot a specific time for each task, it is easier to channel all your energy and focus on that one thing. Finish it and then move on to the next one.

The default diary will represent your quarterly goals, which we will cover in chapter 3. I recommend starting the default diary by breaking your quarterly goals into weekly goals and creating the diary week by week. Then, once you get into the habit of following the weekly diary, begin creating a quarterly diary. I strongly recommend starting with a weekly diary because following this system is very difficult at first; you need to gradually develop it into a habit before moving on to the quarterly diary.

The idea of the default diary is to ensure you are driving your business forward every day and not getting distracted by unimportant tasks. Therefore, it is crucial to have at least 30 minutes dedicated to each day's start or end to plan for that day or the next to know what tasks you are doing. By implementing this, it keeps you focused and allows you to start working straight away.

Your diary shouldn't be all about work. Assign some blocks to spend time with your family and friends too. If you need some time to relax by yourself, put it in as well. You do not have to sacrifice any segment of your life for another unnecessarily. Not all tasks are urgent, and not all are important. You need to identify which tasks are essential for your business growth. Creating a business plan is never urgent, but it is crucial. Segregate the tasks and fulfill the ones that are urgent and save time for the important tasks.

How To Structure Your Default Diary?

All your quarterly, daily, and weekly goals go into your default diary so that you are dedicating specific time to them. Otherwise, you are constantly fixing issues and never working on your business. Your team needs to be fully aware when you are working on essential tasks so that they don't disturb you and need to be aware when you have dedicated time toward problem-solving with your team, so they address all issues or questions with you in these times. We will discuss how to plan your goals in the next chapter; you will then put this all into action in your own business.

The tasks with the highest priority should be attended to first. Then, plan and complete them to avoid chaos later on. You should dedicate a section for business development, recruiting, and pre-planning your business decisions. If any business tasks need your attention, check on them outside of your priority time slot by keeping free spaces for tasks that come up unknowingly. Then, instead of panicking about what to do, you can revisit them in those slots.

Don't be under the impression that creating your default diary is a waste of time, as following this working method will save you a lot of it and make you more productive than any of your competitors. In addition, it will help you get shit done.

THE 80/20 RULE

We are all aware of the Pareto principle, also called the 80/20 rule. It says that 80% of your results are derived from only 20% of your actions. Business is the game of numbers, and when you understand which 20% of your actions are driving most of your results, the outcome is phenomenal. It applies to your personal life as well. You must have seen that only a small percentage of your loyal customers are responsible for the majority of your revenue. The same goes for your business strategies. 80% of your sales are from 20% of your product or services.

What does it mean, and why should you be aware of the 20% activities? Well, if you know which aspect of your business is driving 80% of your results, you could adjust your business to focus all your efforts to elevate the 20% of tasks. What do you think the outcome will be? Exponential growth! So, from today onwards, no matter what you do, ask yourself, which 20% of your activities result in 80% of your gains? Your answer is where you should spend most of your time.

WORK ON YOUR BUSINESS

Michael Gerber presented the theory of working ON your business rather than IN your business in his book *the e-myth*. The E in the book stands for <u>E</u>ntrepreneur. Being a business owner, you should utilize your time working ON your business. Do not get me wrong, working IN your business is also essential. These are the daily tasks of prospecting, fulfilling an order, running the software, etc. However, you should hire people to work in your business so that your time is free to make more significant business decisions that will take you towards your ultimate goals. Hire team members to do the jobs taking your attention away from the tasks that will drive your business forward. Working IN your business refers to the execution and also the management of the execution.

Nevertheless, working ON your business is a strategic approach. It primarily includes establishing various tactics and strategies for your business; like planning, research and development, system creation and implementation, finance, partnerships, decisiveness, etc. As time progresses, while you introduce new products to expand your reach, you also need to create specific systems that will run the business fluently without interrupting the already entrenched business model.

On the contrary, working IN your business dictates carrying out the set activities. It includes every ounce of work you put in to create the product/service, deliver it, and retain customers. Upper-level executives in your organization are responsible for the execution phase. On the top of my head, creating the actual product, administrator tasks, recruiting, marketing, sales, etc., are great examples of working IN your business.

Most business owners get stuck in the business and thus complain that their business isn't growing. Instead, turn the tables and work ON your business so that your employees take care of your daily processes while you are looking at the bigger picture.

You need the skill of goal setting, which is ultimately the key metric to deciding which habits to develop and what action to take. Every business owner should master the art of goal setting and impart it to everyone around him. You're in luck as I've dedicated an entire chapter to this topic. You don't need to thank me. Let's hop on to chapter three and learn everything there is about setting goals and achieving them.

CHAPTER THREE

GOAL SETTING

"If you want to be happy, set a goal that commands your thoughts, liberates your energy, and inspires your hopes."

— Andrew Carnegie

Visionaries are blessed with the skills of foresight. They know who they are, and they implant specific habits into their lives to back up their visions. Being a business owner, you should be well aware of your ultimate goal and where you want your business to be. It is essential to construct both business and personal development goals. Where do you see yourself in the next five years, a decade or two? Did you know that only 5% of the people in the world have goals? Most people have dreams and wishful thinking, but only a few dare to set clear goals for themselves and their businesses. Goal setting is deciding what you want to accomplish and devising a plan to achieve desired results. For entrepreneurs, goal setting is an essential part of business planning.

Life is like a roller coaster; your goals are the runways. If you don't know where you are going, you will never reach the final destination. For instance, pretend that you are invited to an old friend's wedding. It's a destination wedding, and in the midst, you lost the address to the venue. What are your chances of making it to the wedding? Good luck explaining to your friend why you were driving from one place to another in the middle of the night. The goal keeps you on track and enables you and your team to understand what you've achieved. You will be able to track and evaluate your performance report, and it will also allow you to see where you have slacked or not performed and why? Goals and performances should be discussed in meetings and be part of each team member's KPIs. "*All who have accomplished great things have had a great aim, have fixed their gaze on a goal which was high, one which sometimes seemed impossible.*" – Orison Swett Marden.

THE POWER OF VISUALIZATION

Everything starts with a dream. Your business is an awesome example of a dream you saw for yourself; running a business, helping other people with your product and services, becoming financially stable, employing people, and positively impacting the world. Everything begins with a dream. Your motivation could be different than mine, and that's OK. Whatever keeps you going is acceptable. Dreams should be extravagant; they should be so big that they scare you at first. However, they should also be planned and measured to be achievable. You need to dream first and visualize yourself achieving your goals to trick your brain into obtaining them. Your body follows your mind; you decide and create your reality.

Visualization is one of the most powerful tools of the mind. It deceives us into bringing the things we think about into the real world. Great achievers never picture themselves failing or committing a grave mistake, not before their big performance at least; because it increases the likelihood of perpetrating their vision. Visualization techniques train your mind to perform at the highest level, and your mind then proceeds to create new neural pathways to support your reality and help you reach your goal.

Creating a solid mental image of you winning is all there is to visualization. The fact that your mind can think about anything is proof that you should imagine your success to become triumphant in business and life. Imagine it like a simulator that enables you to predict the future. However, it's also a double-edged sword because if you falsely imagine yourself failing out of anxiety, the likelihood of that is also exponential. Conversely, imagining yourself as a winner, a master, one who is destined for success, is a sign that you are using the power of visualization to the highest degree. It isn't arrogant to see yourself as the winner; it is preparation for what's coming – it makes you a very tough competitor to beat.

Let's put this to the test: imagine you're invited to give a speech in front of 2500 people. You've never done it before, and it sends chills down your spine. That's perfectly alright. You've already memorized the speech, but the thought of speaking in front of that many people is unsettling for you. Under these circumstances, you relax your mind and sit quietly with your eyes closed. You visualize yourself on the stage wearing a polished and sharp outfit. There is a happy crowd of 5000 people, and all eyes are on you. You walk in the centre under the limelight and start your speech. The spotlight is where things get pretty interesting. You will mess up the first time, second, or even the first 100 times.

At first, your expressions wouldn't be that good. Maybe your starting hook isn't that powerful, perhaps you stutter at some part, or maybe your closure doesn't hold the required punch. You will get the evaluation of your performance through visualization. When you keep repeating yourself walking down the stage and delivering a speech, you will evidently see yourself speaking in front of 5000 people and make them excited to listen.

I asked you to imagine 5000 people because when you imagine a double crowd, you won't break a sweat when you walk in front of 2500 people – you will be flawless in reality because you've been practicing it in your mind. Seeing yourself succeed increases your confidence and boosts your morale. It helps you to practice until you gain excellence. Amazing, isn't it?

Now, I know you are excited and probably wondering how to visualize correctly. No need to be surprised; I can read minds! It's a simple step-by-step process. Here it goes:

1. **Aim for the moon**: It's a crucial visualization element because you cannot determine true success without gaining an outcome. So, first, clearly decide what you want the outcome to be.

2. **Sit and imagine**: Sit alone in a quiet environment away from distractions so that you can focus entirely on this exercise. Picture a scene where you already have the outcome you imagined. Remember the public speaking example I gave you before? In the same way, use your mind to emulate your success and provide you with what you want.

3. **Picture the details**: The power lies in the clarity and details. The clearer the image, the more realistic and believable it appears to you. For example, let's extend the previous example. When presenting a speech, picture the stage, the color of drapes, the suit you're wearing, shoes, accessories, audience, and everything. Keep it authentic.

4. **Repeat daily**: Visualization is a significant habit, and you cannot expect results in one attempt. Instead, you need to practice it daily, and each time, make the image clearer and more detailed, to a point where it becomes a replica of real life.

Have you ever planned any goals in your business and personal life? And if you have, are you on track with them? What are they? How far are you from achieving them? If you have not achieved any of your goals yet, then it is probably because they are not fully measurable, and you have not visualized yourself achieving them. So, here's a task for you: write a list of goals you would like to accomplish in the next 90 days. This list will help you to begin the process. Once you've decided what you want, you should go ahead and set a specific time every day to indulge in visualization.

VISION BOARD

I've seen a significant difference in the magnitude of success when people go a level beyond and use another powerful tool to influence their power of visualization. It's called a vision board. Create a vision board so that you are reminded every day where you are heading. The vision board is an extremely powerful tool; it helps you keep your goals and dreams in the back of your mind all the time. They allow you to have a clear vision and image of where you want to go or what you want to accomplish, and they help you believe it is possible. The way it works is that you could pin all your dreams onto the board and look at it every day. It keeps your goals fresh and forces you to imagine them.

Keep it simple...

Most people have an infinite number of dreams to achieve, but they are sunk deep into the sea of ambiguity and never surface. Since they don't remind themselves about their dreams, the likelihood of achieving those dreams is pretty low. Most new year's resolutions are forgotten by February; only a very small percentage of people carry out their commitments throughout the year. Successful people like Steve Harvey, Oprah Winfrey, Richard Brandson, Ellen DeGenerous, Beyonce, Lilly Singh, and many more. They all understand the magnetic power that the vision board holds.

It attracts your dreams into reality. Turn your phone and other devices into a vision board if you have to, keep images of your dreams as your wallpaper, background, screensavers, on the wall, and anything you could get your eyes on. A vision board enhances clarity; you know you want to buy a Rolls Royce when you stick a stunning image of it onto the wall. Vision board proponent Jack Canfield said, "*Your brain will work tirelessly to achieve the statements you give your subconscious mind. And when those statements are the affirmations and images of your goals, you are destined to achieve them.*"

Have you ever wondered how beautiful your life would be if you had a magic lamp that fulfills wishes? I see that smile on your face. Fortunately, you do have a magic lamp in your possession. Hold on; you don't have to destroy your closet to find it; it's within your grasp – your brain. Your mind is designed to support you and fulfill your wishes. It has specific rules, though. It only helps you when you constantly command it to get you something. The more you ask your brain for something, the more chances you have of getting it, which is why people who surround themselves with negativity never stay happy in their life because they train their brains to relive all the horrors of the past and make their present miserable.

On the other hand, optimists who are full of energy and bond with everyone positively stay happy and smiling forever because they have trained their minds to be cheerful, happy and optimistic. It's a very simple equation; you get what you say *repeatedly*. It works on the law of attraction.

SMART GOALS

George Doran introduced the concept of S.M.A.R.T goals along with Arthur Miller and James Cunningham in their 1981 article titled, "There's a S.M.A.R.T. way to write management goals and objectives." It will revolutionize your method of goal setting and help you achieve them. So, let's explore it in further detail. S.M.A.R.T means Specific, Measurable, Achievable, Relevant, and Time-bound.

1. **Specific**: Your goal should be simple, clear, and specific; otherwise, you won't be able to focus your efforts or feel truly motivated to achieve the goal. For instance, if you want to become an author just like Shannon, then your specificity will look like this: *I will write a book of 30,000 words on the topic of business growth in the next two months*. When drafting your goal, try to answer the five "W" questions (According to mindtools.com):
   - What do I want to accomplish?
   - Why is this goal important?
   - Who is involved?
   - Where is it located?
   - Which resources or limits are involved?

2. **Measurable**: Unmeasured goals are the ones that are never accomplished. If you want to achieve your goals, you first need to make them measurable. Don't go crazy and set a goal that cannot be achieved. It's obscene to say

that you will earn $1 million in revenue in the first month of starting your business. For example, your measurable goal could be making $1 million in revenue in the first 24 months. That's around $41,666 per month. It is far more achievable, and at the same time, it will push you out of your comfort zone.

3. **Achievable:** Your goal must be accurate and attainable. It must enhance your abilities and yet remain possible to achieve. For example, you may realize that you only made $20,000 in a month, and it was one of the best months of your business history. Therefore, you need to extend your timeline, expand your business, make it efficient, and match the monthly revenue with the goal during such times.

4. **Relevant:** Making sure that your goal is relevant is also essential. Don't set a $1 million revenue goal when you're far away from setting a distribution channel, marketing, and hiring a few people to handle the delivery. Revenue isn't relevant when your business isn't fully ready for the market. Prioritize them first and once everything falls into perspective, then set goals for expansion.

5. **Time-Bound:** A goal without a deadline takes way longer to accomplish than it should. Make it a habit of writing a date beside a goal so that you can value your commitment and stay on track to fulfill the promises you make to yourself. You may have noticed that I mentioned

the 24-month deadline for a million-dollar revenue and reverse-engineered the goal into monthly checkpoints, didn't you? That is the time-bound technique where if I hadn't mentioned installing a timeline, the revenue goal would take forever to reach the desired mark.

QUARTERLY PLANNING

"Our goals can only be reached through a vehicle of a plan, in which we must fervently believe, and upon which we must vigorously act. There is no other route to success." – Pablo Picasso. You must have started the business with a vision; what is it? Always keep the end goal in mind. It is great to climb a building one stair at a time, but what if you're climbing the wrong building? That's how important your final vision is. Making a boatload of money is not a real goal (it could be for some people, but the actual fulfillment is leaving a legacy behind); it is just a driving entity.

Your real purpose should be something more significant than that. It should affect you, the people around you, and the entire world. Tesla's vision is not to make the coolest cars; although they do, their real vision is to help people transition to electric vehicles so that we don't run out of non-renewable resources. Write down your end goal for your business. Affirm it to yourself and your employees. What is your goal five years or ten years from now?

Break it down to yearly, quarterly, weekly, and daily goals to achieve your ultimate vision. For example, if your vision is to have 10,000 stores in the next five years, you know you have to set up 2000 stores every year, 500 stores every quarter, or almost six stores every day - this is how you reverse engineer and get your numbers straight. Next, it's time you plan the next 90 days in your business, which is just the first step towards your end goal. Finally, you can use the following steps to create consequent quarterly goals for your business.

Step 1: Embrace Possibilities

Nothing is impossible; along with a dedicated team, you could take on the world. No wall is too high and the bridge too long. Believe in yourself, trust the people who tag along with you, and know that you can attain anything you set your mind to – do not limit yourself in any way. Your hands do not belong within the shackles; they are meant to break chains and explore the horizons. *"When you have no fear, the possibilities are endless."* – Jeffree Star.

Step 2: Create a Vision

What would you like it to be if you and your team can achieve anything in the next 90 days? Record your vision, explain it to your team, add a pinch of emotions, and you are ready to roll. *"Vision is the art of seeing what is invisible to others."* – Jonathan Swift.

Step 3: Pick Key Priorities

Look at your vision and list down the three most critical key tasks that will take you towards your vision. These three goals are the ones you will be focusing keenly on in the next 90 days. Be aware of what you are doing and choose wisely. *"Success is the progressive realization of a worthy goal or ideal."* – Earl Nightingale. Some activities may only happen once, while some need to be done every week. Put all deadlines and tasks into your default diary, make space for these top priority tasks every day. You should be working on these tasks most of your time. They are usually around marketing, sales, driving money into the business, and recruitment. You should be scouting for people for your team every week, which will be discussed in detail in chapter 5. A brilliant CEO or entrepreneur hires great people. People make businesses successful or kill them.

Step 4: Take Consistent Actions

Your major question should be: What are the key actions I must take or focus on consistently to make this priority inevitable? Your goals, habits, and success are results of consistency. Take massive action without giving up, and no force in the universe could stop you from getting what belongs to you. *"Being persistent may lead you to the door, but it is the key that unlocks it."* – Kenny Dasinger.

Step 5: Preview Weekly

The only way to check whether you are on track is to examine your progress against the threshold. Every week, set a time to measure your success and analyze how many goals you achieved from that week, how many tasks you ticked off the checklist. *"Tracking my progress and missteps is one of the reasons I've accumulated the success I have."* – Darren Hardy.

Step 6: Your Daily Plan

Ask yourself this question daily: what are the three critical business tasks that I need to accomplish today to move forward? If you prioritize accurately and fulfill those tasks daily, then by the end of 90 days, you will have your goal within your grasp. Kudos to that!

Tips to Organize Your Day

Consistency is the key to success; here are a few tasks that you should be willing to take on daily:

- Create a daily prioritized to-do list a night prior to or before you open emails first thing in the morning.
- Set a time each week to review the tasks you have and haven't accomplished. Analyze the unfinished tasks and also the reason why they weren't completed. It will also decrease recurrence.
- Start with the most challenging task first.
- Pick and prioritize the three most important tasks.

- These tasks should all be added to your default diary.

These six steps will account for a successful quarter. Once you feel the satisfaction and enjoy it, follow the same steps every quarter, and slowly you will achieve your final vision.

My main goal for starting my temping agency was to run it remotely, leave the UK, earn an income from my business while traveling and build a remote working business to provide that opportunity for other people. I planned to achieve it by the time I received my British passport, which was a 3-year time frame from the start of my business.

When I received my passport, I was already on that journey; I was six months in, left the country, hired my first support team member, and had a team of around 40 contractors working under my company name. When setting this goal at the beginning of my business, I was the one and only contractor in my business. I envisioned my end goal and then broke it down into various time frames (quarterly, monthly, weekly, and daily) until it was achieved; after achieving this goal, I reassessed my business and life and created new goals. What's your purpose?

THE SUCCESS PLAN

When you plan, it should be for absolute success. I was thinking of a big bang to end this chapter, and what better way than showcasing a successful roadmap that will help you achieve your quarterly goals and play an essential part in your overall victory. You seem excited, do you want to know? Of course, you do! I wouldn't refer to it as a step-by-step process to success. Instead, I look at it as a master key to all businesses out there, including yours. I will lend you the key, and I expect you to use it wisely. If you can utilize the master key to unseal the right lock, you will witness the doors of opportunities opening for you.

1. **Live your future life**: It's ironic to think about, but you do have the power to imagine your future, and if you could do that, what is stopping you from living it? I am not talking about buying a five-million-dollar mansion. If you see yourself living in a mansion, that will be a disaster for businesses' growth (the capital will be better spent investing into the growth of your business). Instead, I want you to know what you would do if you were the person you wanted to be and do just that. The decisions you would make, the lifestyle you would live, the things you would do, all of that. You are not to upgrade your living expenses; you should instead upgrade your perspective to the more successful and happier version of yourself. Think like the millionaire you are destined to be, and you will hit the milestone sooner than anticipated – be the change all the time.

2. **Focus on your desires**: Human needs are endless. There is no saying where we would stop if you do not get a hold of yourself. There is nothing wrong with wanting to have everything. However, I don't want you to clutter your mind with all wants at once. Instead, focus on one thing at a time, achieve it, and then plan for the next one. One way makes you a wishful thinker, while the other way makes you a high achiever – your choice. When you focus only on victory, your mind automatically looks for creative ways to achieve success.

3. **Take massive action:** Talk is cheap and holds no value unless you can back it up with success. Where I come from, success is only attracted to those who dare to take massive strategic actions towards their set goals. Action may be the place where you take too long to decide because of the risk of failure, but the loss of delay is inevitable. If you get your facts straight and numbers right, do not waste another fraction of a second thinking about it. Charge in, have faith, and you will triumph.

4. **Do not settle**: Have higher standards for yourself, and do not let anyone talk you out of your goals. You deserve nothing but the best, and you have no reason to settle down for mediocrity. Go for what you want, and don't stop until you achieve it. You are responsible for your success in life. If you want something as badly as you want to breathe and you're determined to work hard

enough to attain it, you will achieve it. The key to success is never to stop; the only failure is "stopping". You are built for affluence; get in gear and drive past the stop signals.

**Here's a small task for you. Write down the list of things you want to achieve both within your business and personal life, and use it as a driving factor every day to help you achieve your goals. There are no limits to your dreams; you are your only limitation. So, dream big and work toward making it happen from the tools I've introduced you to in this chapter.

5. **Build a personal list**: Create a vision and value list for your personal life. Use this list to be your driving factor for daily decisions and for the kind of people you wish to surround yourself with. If someone does not align with your core value system, they are not someone you should surround yourself with. There is a saying that "*we are the five people we surround ourselves with*," so be very selective. We can't choose our family or blood relatives, but we can choose our friends and partners – be wise.

That was an amazing journey so far, and we are finally entering into the lane of a differentiator. In the next chapter, you will learn about the core values and company culture. Being a leader, you should always strive to build a great place for your people to work in harmony. The upcoming chapter is designed to help you achieve just that. I must say that you look ready. I do not want to keep you waiting any longer; let's move!

CHAPTER FOUR

CORE VALUES AND CULTURE

"Corporate culture matters. How management chooses to treat its people impacts everything for better or for worse."

— Simon Sinek

Running a business is a difficult job. You wear many hats and try everything in your power to make it a delightful experience for everyone who's involved. Business owners focus all their energy on customers and make them the whole and soul while neglecting their true drivers — employees. Famous entrepreneurs like Tony Hsieh, Richard Branson, indulge in making their employees have a great experience in their business. Employees spend half of their lives in your business to help make your dream come true. Of course, they take money from your pocket, but they are also why you have that money in the first place. So, where am I going with this? A thriving business that everybody loves, from employees to customers, is only possible when you have the foundational aspects in check: your organization's core values and company culture.

Good culture makes people stick with you for the long haul, while a negative culture repels them to seek another offer. As a leader, it is your primary duty to straighten up your core values and make them an unbreakable code of conduct that doesn't flex even for you. When you have core values in place, you reveal them during your recruitment process and hire only those who align with your company values. This chapter is dedicated to helping you build a solid culture for your business that is engaging, coachable, and productive. Gary Vaynerchuck said that *"Company culture is the backbone of any successful organization."* You can't hire and lead a team if you don't have a company culture in place. The culture, vision, and values lead the direction of your business. You hire people who fit into these elements, or you don't hire them at all, regardless of their shiny resumes and skills.

IMPORTANCE OF COMPANY VISION

A vision statement is a direct sentence that relates where the company aspires to be in the upcoming years. This statement reveals the "where" of a business, meaning the direction a business is trying to go and what type of impact you wish to have upon others. The difference between mission and vision statements lies in the purpose they serve. A vision statement is essential for a company because, without it, you as a leader and everyone who follows you, will have absolutely no sense of direction. If you have no vision, then why are you doing business in the first place? Where are you going? Money is only a by-product of the value you provide in the marketplace and the problems you solve. It is never the vision of a company to have more money.

You already know what a vision is; it's the mental image of your desired future. However, if it isn't written well on a piece of paper, it holds no value for your employees because they can't read your mind. They have no idea what goes inside your brain and what your intentions are regarding the business. Therefore, to bring clarity and inspire everyone to join in, you should introduce a vision statement that signifies every aspect of your business in the future. Your employees should quickly tell what their purpose is in the business by that one statement. It should be impactful and verbally accessible. John Graham explained it like this, "*You've got to give yourself the freedom to dream – to use your imagination to see and feel what does not yet exist. A vision is not the same as goals or objectives; those come from the head. A vision comes from the heart.*"

Your burning passion and dreams influence your vision. You integrate reality to create a far better future for you, your employees, and your customers. Let me give you three major aspects of how a vision should be:

1. **It should unite**: Company's vision should unify all those who work on it. People should come together and work on a single mission. Your most significant task will be making everyone believe that they are a crucial part of a bigger meaningful picture.

2.   **It must inspire**: Nobody likes to work for a business that doesn't inspire them at an individual level. You must give your staff more than just monetary value in exchange for their faith, loyalty, and sweat. Being a visionary, I instantly grasped how important it would be for my business if I wanted my people to happily do more than 100% every day for its growth. It must impact everyone and project a symbol of energy and enthusiasm. It especially counts when things aren't going too great. At the peak, everyone is excited and working to their best ability, but the vision inspires them to keep going without having second thoughts during the fall.

3.   **It must have one outcome**: Having a vision allows you to have one focal point to focus your entire effort. It is a risky trade if your business offers all of the services because then it is a jack of all trades but a master of none. Whereas, when you know your niche, you are aware of your vision, it empowers you and your team to work in harmony at the highest level – one purpose, one direction, one outcome, and no turning back. So let your ambitions run wild.

MISSION STATEMENT V/S VISION STATEMENT

A mission statement clarifies what the company actually wants to achieve, who they want to support, and why they want to support them. Conversely, a vision statement describes where the company wants to be in the mere future. Thus, a mission statement is a roadmap for the company's vision statement. It's the difference between today and tomorrow.

Mission statement is a literal quote stating what a brand or company is setting out to accomplish. It enables the public to know about the product and service, who they are for, and why they exist. Conversely, a vision statement is a brand looking toward the future and saying what it hopes to achieve through its mission statement. The vision statement is more conceptual, as it's a glimpse into what the brand can become in the eyes of the consumer and the value it will bring in longevity.

The mission statement of the company cannot change. It remains the same for the most part. However, the vision statement could certainly change because there can always be a new place the company could be headed towards, but its mission and what it does for its consumers cannot be changed.

Vision Statement

It's essential to have both mission and vision statements because one is dependent on the other to sustain. A company's mission, purpose, goals, and values are all involved in creating a company's vision. You can always seek inspiration from your competitor, discern their vision statement, and try to stand out from the crowd. The vision statement increases exponentially when it's concise; don't make it longer than two sentences. Make it meaningful and encourage hope in the hearts of all your employees to memorize it and repeat it. More importantly, they should understand it and believe that it has the possibility of being a reality. Hold on! Before moving forward, you need to have a vision statement of your own. Here are 8 tips to help you craft a meaningful vision statement today:

- Project five to 10 years in the future and jot it down.
- Dream big and focus on success.
- Write it in the present tense.
- Use clear, concise, jargon-free language.
- Infuse it with passion and make it inspiring.
- Align it with your business values and goals.
- Create a plan to communicate your vision statement to your employees.
- Prepare to commit time and resources to the vision you establish.

My recruitment business vision statement was: Happy Therapist - Happy Spa - Happy Client. The mission around this vision *was to ensure therapists were put first, that they were happy and well paid, and in return, the spa clients would be happy, well looked after, which meant our clients would be satisfied with our services. Our goal was to ensure that spa therapists were paid what they deserved because in the UK, spa therapists were severely underpaid at the time.*

Your vision statement describes how the world will look if you achieve your mission. Think aspirationally and describe the ideal end state. Key questions to consider are as follows:

- What role in the world do we want this organization to play?
- What is the idealized future state we want to create?
- How will people live differently if our organization is successful?

Go ahead, try out a bunch of vision statements and finalize the one you believe to be the absolute fit for your business. It is very important to train your staff towards the organization's destination.

Mission Statement

According to Investopedia, "a company's mission statement defines its culture, values, ethics, fundamental goals, and agenda. In addition to that, it defines how each of these applies to the company's stakeholders — like its suppliers, employees, distributors, shareholders, and the community at large. Use this statement to align their goals with that of the company. The statement reveals what the company does, how it does it, and why it does it." When you start to bring in new investors, they will look at your mission statement and match it with their ethics. If it aligns, they will be happy to team up with you. For instance, an investor who doesn't believe in gambling would never invest his money in casinos. It's just against his policy. Hence, the way you structure your mission statement is crucial.

It may sound challenging at first, but there are a few steps to help you create a compelling mission statement. The first and one of the most important steps is knowing what your business does. It is an ironically bitter truth that most business owners are unaware of which industry they are dealing in. For instance, a soft foam hat company might think that they are in the foam hat-making business, while in reality, they are in the fun and gig sharing business. If you are unclear about the industry, your business caters to, conduct thorough research to find out. You cannot proceed without knowing this crucial element of your business.

Once you understand the "what," the next step is finding the "how." Meaning, you should then outline how your business operates and achieves the envisioned results. Don't be technical and list down the software and techniques; instead, draw out how you provide value to your customers. For example, when you are selling a soft mattress, your value is *a night of better sleep*, not the best quality of materials. Know the difference!

The final step is to understand the "why" of your business. Why do you do what you do? For example, suppose you're running a business to aid cancer. In that case, it's because someone from your family or friends suffered severely from this disease, and now you are on a mission to make this world a better place for cancer patients because you know how painful it is for people and their families.

Now, combine all the above steps. You will have a fantastic mission statement that will inspire your employees to willingly work twice as hard and for your customers to know precisely what your company does and the value it offers – clarity, position, and growth, three birds with one stone. Here are a few examples of mission statements from some of the biggest giants of the market:

- **Microsoft**: Empower every person and organization on the planet to achieve more.
- **Nike**: To bring inspiration and innovation to every athlete in the world.
- **Walmart**: We save people money so they can live better.
- **Starbucks**: To inspire and nurture the human spirit— one person, one cup, and one neighborhood at a time.
- **Tesla**: To accelerate the world's transition towards sustainable energy.

- **JP Morgan**: To be the best financial services company in the world.

To sum up, when you are on the journey towards success and growth, you need the immense support of the vision and the strength of the mission. Combine these two, and your business will know no bounds. Therefore, answer the following questions and create your mission statement before moving forward.

- What is our overarching intent as an organization?
- What makes us different from everyone else?
- What is the essence of what we're trying to achieve?

CORE VALUES

The values we hold dear to our organization cannot be sacrificed under any circumstance. Having strong core values drives the business forward. It demonstrates what employees should value and adhere to individually. Core values support your vision, shape the culture, and reflect the essence of the company. It's your identity, the principles you follow, your belief system, and your philosophy; all are integrated to form your values. Technical competencies enable the business transition, but your core values are the underlying competencies that empower the company to run smoothly. Establish strong foundational values as it protects your business both internally and externally.

Your core values help you in the decision-making process. Since they are rigid unbreakable rules, you will not make any decision in your business that violates your values. For example, one of the core values of the Rolls Royce company is the handmade quality of the product. They will never, under any circumstances, launch an inferior product. On the contrary, they take pride in their quality. After extensive, rigorous testing, if they find even a minor fault, they discard the launch and fix it immediately—no wonder the majority of their models are still running on the roads after decades.

In a world where most businesses are booming with similarities, having core values makes you stand out from the crowd and directly connect with your customers, potential clients, investors, employees, and stakeholders. It clarifies your identity and distances the people who do not align with them. For instance, if you're running a law firm that operates on the value of providing justice to innocent people against criminals, do you think vicious people will have the audacity to enter your office and seek help to commit a crime and get away with it? Of course not. *"My definition of success: When your core values and self-concept are in harmony with your daily actions and behaviors."* – John Spence.

Furthermore, your values are the most critical recruiting and retention tools for your business. People who do not align with them should never be recruited in the first place, no matter how good their degrees are, and the people who break or lose faith in your values shouldn't be kept around. It damages your reputation. It is easier than ever to research a company from the comfort of home; job seekers do their homework before applying. The clearer you highlight your core value, the less hassle you have to go through during recruitment. If it is your first attempt at drafting your company values, use your personal principles as a guide to creating your company values. Your business values should align with your own values.

As time passes, your employees need a reason to believe in you and your company. At first, when joining your company, they are enthusiastic and excited about the change, but as time passes, the excitement fades. Having strong core values will give them a reason to believe in your business and work hard to keep it that way for a long time. They are the heart and soul of your goal-setting process. When organizing quarterly, yearly, and future goals of your business, you must also prioritize your core values and set your goals accordingly. Everything revolves around your values - your employees should embody them.

Creating Core Values

Most people mistake their core values for single words such as Integrity, commitment, quality, etc., but these are vague terms and not as impactful. One word is not enough. You need a statement and then explain that statement to gain clarity. For instance, if your core value is Integrity, you could describe it as *"we act with Integrity.* We are honest, we never backstab our friends, we are accountable for our actions, and we analyze the impact."

When creating your core values, you need to stay away from aspirational values because they are theoretical and unreal. Core values should be the very nature of your company. Your business shouldn't contradict your own values because your entire system is built upon these values. Hence, do not confine them to just your website. Bring them into practice, walk the talk. List down all the values your company will never compromise for; it can include your strongest belief and the unique experience you provide. You will reach your core values when you know what you stand for and what is more important to your employees, customers, and stakeholders. Your company values will engage your employees and, in turn, shape your culture.

When you come up with concrete core values, make sure that everyone in your company knows and believes in them. Then, let them embed the values into their behaviors, and **you** are part of your team; therefore, the same rules apply to you. Lead by example.

BUILDING A POSITIVE COMPANY CULTURE

An effective leader like you should invest heavily into building a positive, engaging, and productive culture that inspires your employees to work more efficiently. *"You can have all the right strategies in the world; if you don't have the right culture, you're dead."* – Patrick Whitesell. The company culture is an integral part of your business. It impacts the organization's attributes, from recruiting top performers to enhancing overall work satisfaction.

A bland, negative culture will pressure the employees to struggle and lose faith in the mission or vision. It is crucial that you define a specific culture and then hire people who meet those guidelines. A wrong culture fit with a shiny resume is a liability. In contrast, the right culture fit with average skill could be improved with training and become a phenomenal asset to the organization. You need to see these things and understand that business is not only about finding great people to work with; it's about discerning the **right people** with whom you do not have to try to get along. It should happen effortlessly because you all value the same things. When starting, you cannot risk getting someone who does not fit in the bigger picture; trust me, you will always have problems if that is the case. Culture is the backbone for happy workdays and long-lasting relationships.

Company culture can be fun, serious, adventurous, exciting, travel friendly, or anything you want it to be. All you have to do is find that theme and stick with it forever. For example: if you choose a travel-friendly theme, all the employees and recruits must love traveling. Maybe yours is a remote working team, and you meet in different countries every year for team building. Anyone who isn't comfortable with traveling and prefers staying in their home city, town, or country wouldn't be the best fit for this company culture because they would be uncomfortable packing their bags and flying for meet-ups.

Our company provides an allowance to work in different workspaces worldwide; we believe in external stimulation to keep our employees motivated. Therefore, we encourage them to work in workspaces of their choice. It is a company's requirement to work in a coworking space twice a week for external motivation. Anyone who doesn't like this idea wouldn't sit well with our company culture, therefore, would eventually leave our company. Creating a company culture is to avoid precisely that − a high turnover of staff; that stuns the growth and is extremely expensive for a small business during the scaling-up process.

Zappos is an online shoe and clothing retailer company that succeeded because of its culture. They embrace the diversity and uniqueness of every individual in their company, thus standing out from the crowd. They are heavily invested in their culture and protect it with everything they've got. They even announced that the success they have today is because of the culture and *zapponians* (their employees).

Culture embarks creativity from every department; for example, their finance department has reconstructed a haunted house used as their Las Vegas headquarters offices. You read it right; their creativity is off the charts. Just imagine, if their finance department was capable of creating this idea, what are the limitations of their marketing team? NONE! Their company mission is *to "deliver wow" by turning "unwows" into "wows."* They are fun, unique, and sometimes a little irreverent. Their customer service representative has the same rights as the CEO to help the customers who call and complain. They don't mess around with their culture; they take it seriously. They give away $2000 for recruits to quit, who complete the induction training and find the culture to be unfit - that's a heavy investment. They have over 1500 employees and more than $2 billion in revenue. I hope this story has sparked some ideas about culture and how to build one for your company.

We will dive into detail about the recruitment process in the next chapter; however, for now, you must understand that it will be extremely detrimental and expensive for a small business if you end up with the wrong people. You need a solid foundation, which can only be achieved with people who align with your culture.

Employees feel great and perform at their best when provided with a positive, healthy, and growth environment. If you can turn your office into *the best place to work*, you will have one hell of a team backing you up. Your culture is the overall mixture of mission, beliefs, vision, and behavior. Every interaction in the business is a result of your culture. Define what is admissible and what's not upfront. No one has the right to destroy your culture, not even you.

Recruitment is one of the best benefits of having a strong positive culture. You hire the applicants who suit well with your business and discard the ones who don't. It enhances employee loyalty exponentially. If you execute this process fluently, you will find yourself working with almost the same batch of employees for decades. The second benefit is the job satisfaction that people experience on a daily basis. We've seen employees pushed to the level of exhaustion for no reason, and that repels them away.

People who stick around are there only to pay bills as they have no other offers lining up. But they will only shake hands with you until they get selected somewhere else. Dedicated employees who are provided with a great culture, won't mind their salary being 1-2% less than the competition. They will stick with you through thick and thin. It doesn't mean you should provide them with a great culture and cut off their salaries. I mean, that is just an atrocious gesture. Instead, take care of them and make them feel valued. Richard Branson said, *"There's no magic formula for great company culture. The key is just to treat your staff how you would like to be treated."*

A great culture reduces employee stress and burnout. It improves their performances, and also gives rise to a strong interlinked team that collaborates on a greater magnitude and helps overcome any obstacle that steps in between you and your ultimate dream. You can look at the companies who've achieved a thriving company culture; they are now a force to be reckoned with. One of the best things about building a positive culture is that it can be done with any budget, company size, and within any industry. As long as employers take time to invest in their workforce's happiness and well-being, a positive culture will grow and thrive.

HOW TO CREATE A STRONG COMPANY CULTURE

We have learned about the benefits and why you need a great company culture, but in this section, you will learn how to create one in a step-by-step process.

Tips to Building a Positive Culture

I will end this chapter by giving you nine great tips that will help you as a leader build a positive corporate culture in the workplace.

1. **Employee wellness**: Healthy employees should be your top priority as no positive relationship could be fostered between you and them otherwise. Your employees should feel fantastic physically, mentally, and emotionally when they walk into the workplace. Being a leader, it is your responsibility to provide them with the best health care, on-site tools, and resources to encourage them to live healthy, happy lives.

2. **Improve your current culture:** Just because you are in the middle of creating a new culture doesn't mean that you vanquish everything your company stood for until now. Interact with your employees, ask them what they do and don't like, evaluate, and then slowly enhance your culture to the best version. Don't fire all rules at once without consultation because that might scare them away. However, you should also be mindful that whoever doesn't align with your company values and culture will eventually leave during this process. Please don't be sad; it's a good thing because you only need people who fully align with it.

3. **Provide purpose:** It's not enough to have a vision for the business alone; you should also provide your employees with a proper purpose at an individual level within your establishment. Show them that they are valuable and allow them to prove it back to you. Most employees crave validation and value; there is a better chance of job satisfaction for them if you successfully provide them with a purpose.

4. **Create goals:** I haven't seen a positive corporate culture that gets things done without having clear specific goals. How will you evaluate the growth if there is nothing for them to achieve on a daily, weekly, monthly, and yearly basis? Set a clear goal for your business, execute it, and move on to the next one.

5. **Elevate positivity:** Encourage positivity in offices and do whatever you can to accomplish it. Hang some inspirational quotes, hero pictures, your mission statement, and anything that ignites positivity in the environment – do it without a second thought.

6. **Foster meaningful connections:** Relationship in the workplace is very crucial because it empowers teamwork and improves the odds of you making it to the top of the market. When employees barely know their colleagues and rarely interact, there's no possible way for a solid culture to grow. Introduce sessions for them to interact and get to know each other, share

their stories, and where they came from? Teach them to respect other employees, you, and your business through leadership, and they will be an unstoppable team.

7. **Listen well:** I believe that one of the rewarding skills after communication is listening skills. People don't value it much and miss out on some great advice and feedback from their employees and customers. Listen to your employees. It is one of the best ways to make them feel valued.

8. **Identify champions:** There will be employees who embody the culture, mission, and values. They are very excited to promote your aspirations and business values further ahead. Find these people and encourage them to keep spreading the cheers.

9. **Stop pretending:** Just to make yourself look good, don't pretend to be someone you're not. Masks are unforgivable. Your business needs to be built on loyalty, trust, and transparency. So don't pretend to be someone you aren't; it won't last. The day your truth is revealed, it will be a massive hit for your business and you personally. So be who you are and keep improving yourself – that's the safest path.

Be sure to cultivate a positive culture that enhances your workforce's talent, diversity, and happiness. Building a unique, positive culture is one of the best and simplest ways to get your employees to invest their talent and future with your company for the long term.

That takes us to the most paramount question of all: how to recruit a winning team that fulfills your vision and culture? It's time we fold the sleeves and get in there with full force because the next chapter will teach you how to hire a phenomenal team and keep them loyal to you. I see that shine in your eyes. It's about time!

CHAPTER FIVE

HIRING A WINNING TEAM

"Nothing we do is more important than hiring and developing people. At the end of the day, you bet on people, not on strategies."

— Lawrence Bossidy

Building a successful business requires recruiting great people who fit your profile and match your company's culture and values. This chapter will solve your biggest recruitment problems. No more painful decisions for hiring the wrong guy and then letting them go after experiencing loss or dispute. We will use the culture and core values as the primary driving force in our recruitment process. Furthermore, you will also analyze the current team you're working with to examine whether they check all your boxes or were impulse recruits out of urgency for filling those empty seats.

The critical thing to remember about recruiting is hiring a team that will work IN your business for you as the CEO to work ON your business. As the CEO of your business, you need to ensure that you are leading your team; that all team members and departments are falling in line with the company goals and vision. You should create and follow an organizational structure in your business and then hire accordingly.

THE ORGANIZATIONAL STRUCTURE

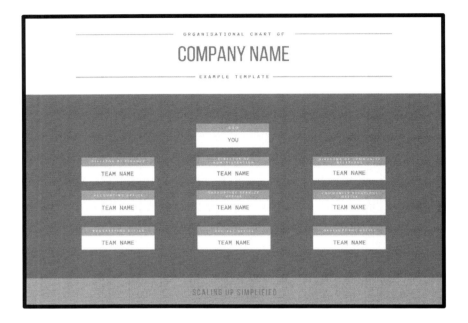

It is a perfect setup for management and operations with key specified roles of every individual in the form of a hierarchical chart. It entails the function of every individual in a detailed way so that there is no confusion between the employees. In the initial days when you are acting in place of multiple positions, there is always a conundrum of who is supposed to do what; the organizational chart will help you ease the process. The chart will highlight all the positions required in your business, like a manager, CFO, technician, marketer, etc. If you are currently a one-person show, you should be writing your name in every position for now.

This way, when someone joins your team, you could easily delegate that position with all the duties. The organizational structure also demonstrates the flow of information as to which position is answerable to whom. There are endless ways a company could be structured; you just have to find the one that suits you best depending on your mission and initiate the process.

Use this structure to start the hiring process because it will allow you to navigate from working IN your business to work ON your business. But, first, you have to decide which tasks are to be performed and assign them to their respective roles so that you can free up your time and work on business growth, strategies and drive your business towards success.

I understand that it can be intimidating when you are unsure of which positions to fill in the initial stages of the recruitment process. To make this process easier, you should take yourself three years into the future and imagine where you see your company. What are the functions required for you, and how will it operate? By doing this, it will provide you with an estimated overview of the business structure. However, don't take yourself too far and set an impossible target; make it sensible and achievable (use chapter 3 for guidance).

Now, after you've set an achievable goal for your business that is pushing you out of your comfort zone, outline what you will need to achieve the vision. After creating the organizational chart, a few roles will be presented before you that will need filling. You could start the process by understanding your strengths and mastering your strengths, and then hiring highly skilled people in all the areas representing your weaknesses. For example, if you are a visionary like me, focus on that and hire experienced people to take care of your finance, marketing, operations, etc. *"The competition to hire the best will increase in the years ahead. Companies that give extra flexibility to their employees will have the edge in this area."* – Bill Gates.

You must understand all the critical functions within your business to drive your business toward success. However, suppose you currently have a limited cash flow available and aren't able to fill all these positions, you can prioritize and hire an administrative assistant who could attend to the admin related tasks within your business, which will free up more of your time so you can focus on growth-related tasks such as marketing, sales, and recruiting. Then, as your company starts to scale and the cash flow increases, you can continue to fill more positions and free up more of your time. As a business owner, your time is valuable – use it wisely on essential tasks that drive your business forward.

If you are still uncertain about which roles to outline in your organizational structure, let me assist you by highlighting the five pivotal functions each company should consist of; they are as follows:

Function 1: Finance

It is one of the most fascinating and vital aspects of your business. You can evaluate your profits and revenue with all the costs. Numbers in business are everything. Understanding the finances in your business will help you assess whether your business is growing or stagnant. The name of the game should be a return on investment, you've poured your blood, sweat, and tears into this business, and you deserve profits. Having enough cash to invest in your business is one of your duties as a CEO (you will learn more about this in chapter 7).

Nonetheless, you should outsource it to an accountant and bookkeeper to ensure that this element of your business is being maintained like a well-oiled machine. When your company grows, you will need a finance department and CFO dedicated to taking care of your business's finances, keeping a regular tab on your outsourced accountants and bookkeepers, and verifying everything. But in the early stages of the "Scaling Up process", an entire finance department is unnecessary.

Function 2: Sales and Marketing

Although these are two different sectors, we will combine them as one in this description for simplicity. Marketing is where the show begins. You create awareness and excitement about your business among the target audience. Good marketing generates leads, whereas the sales team closes the deal and converts the leads into potential customers. Your branding, core values, mission, interest, and problem-solving ability are going to play a significant role in your marketing.

On the other hand, sales work in conjunction with your marketing as interested leads make a purchase, counting as a sale. Marketing is a broad scope, and you should know how many people will be required to carry out the marketing within your business. Every important role goes on your organizational chart. For example, a social media manager won't necessarily manage the SEO within your company. We will discuss more about this in chapter 8.

Function 3: Customer Support and Service

Once your marketing is successful and the sales increase, you will have a growing customer base. Tending to all their needs is what your future growth depends on. The customer support team will need to swiftly attend to your customer's queries and solve their problems. Providing a great experience will allow you to get return business from the customer, building a loyal fan base. Why do you think people line up in front of Apple stores for hours during the launch of new iPhones?

Function 4: Operations

Every process and system executed falls under operations. You need skilled people to use systems and develop great products to ensure quality, efficiency, and capacity; deliver as promised to the customers. Most business owners are visionaries like me and struggle in the operations phase. Therefore, hiring an operations manager should be at the top of your priority list. You could have multiple ideas regarding your business, but you also need someone to hold you accountable and keep you on track until the set goal is accomplished. Your operation manager will take care of daily business operations and make sure that everything runs smoothly. You, as a CEO, should work side by side with them to ensure all timelines are met.

Function 5: Admin and Management

These are vital roles because they include all admin-related tasks, feedback, communication with clients and customers, meetings, etc. It helps you keep your business organized. If you ask me, filling this position should be your first recruitment duty. If you delay hiring an admin manager for your business, you as a CEO will have to spend most of your day dragging through the details and never get to focus on the growth of your business.

Each department needs a manager that oversees all the instructions, systems and processes directed from operations and the CEO. Management will also be responsible for the first stage recruitment and interview process; therefore, they must be trustworthy. You must hire the right people for the right roles. You can't have many visionaries in one business because it will be a business of ideas and no implementation thereof. I can relate to this from my recruitment business.

We were a team of visionaries; therefore, we all presented great ideas in our weekly team meetings, which were forgotten by the time we conducted our next weekly meeting; nothing was executed until we hired an operations manager. You can imagine that it was a recipe for disaster. These five functions are the pillars of your business. So, take special care of them and hire people who could walk the talk.

HIRING ACCORDING TO COMPANY CULTURE

A company's culture is an intangible factor that matters more than you think. It encompasses all the company's notions that dictate how people interact, the bantering style, and everything else is a reward thanks to the culture. A culture fit is a concept screening potential candidates to determine what type of cultural impact they would have on the organization. The examination is performed by considering the values, beliefs, and behaviors that exist between the employee and you.

Hiring people who fit like jigsaw pieces and bring the right balance to your business ensures a great flow of energy. People will work amazingly with each other and get along pretty well. Any new member added to "the pride" should align with the same values and vision; only then could they add more value towards your goals. Before you conduct an interview, make sure you have a list of attributes that qualifies them for your culture – ask many questions and verify all your doubts. Now, go ahead, write down five attributes you are looking for in your employees and use them as a guiding bar in the recruitment process.

Remember, these attributes are the qualities, not their skills. Look for skills only after you've qualified them as a great culture fit. Skills can be taught, but values, respect, hard work, discipline, determination, and a positive attitude cannot be taught. Are you done with the list?

Create An Attractive Job Description

An awesome job description is meant to attract only the most suitable candidates – treat it as a marketing tool that will bring you a pack of pre-qualified candidates. Your employees are just as important or sometimes more important than your clients and customers; it is your duty to treat them as such. The purpose of a great job description is to spread the news about what type of people you are hiring for your business. It is also an excellent way to publish an ad and promote the company.

It is easy to create a fantastic job description; let me show you how. Seven elements need to be present in an effective job description.

1. **A catchy job title:** It is the first thing people notice; therefore, let it stand out from your competitors and ensure that it dictates exactly what you want with a punch – it is your first impression and attraction.
2. **Vision statement:** Begin the job description with your company's vision statement. Let people know who you are and the direction you are headed.
3. **Company culture:** The second section should highlight your company culture, which will attract the

right people. From reading your company's culture, they will feel excited to work for your company as it fundamentally aligns with them.

4.   **Key attributes:** Highlight the key attributes for the role they are applying for, make it clear and concise.

5.   **KPIs for the role:** Every job description should list each role's KPIs (key performance indicator), which will make the candidate aware of the goals and duties required for the position. (To be discussed in further detail, later on in the chapter).

6.   **Skills and qualifications:** Only after mentioning the above sections will you highlight the job's required skills and qualifications.

7.   **Call to action:** This is the most critical section of your job description. For example, you ask the candidate to send a 30-60 seconds video explaining why they want to work for your company and what attracted them to this position. It shouldn't include any of their skills or reasoning about why they are applying. Instead, it should include the character and attributes that match your company culture and vision that excited them the most about the role (tell them where to find your email address; which section of your website). The call to action should be at the end of the job description.

How To Filter Applicants and Save Time?

Now, I can understand if you are thinking, why the video? Well, it ensures that candidates applying have read your entire description and are taking the application seriously. They are not just applying to your company along with 100s of other companies without reading the whole job application. You won't open any CV or job application at this stage who hasn't followed your instructions; you will only watch the video applications. Therefore, you won't be wasting your precious time on the candidates who just sent their CVs and did not follow through. It's a filtering process to gain dedicated candidates. This process will cut the successful applicants from 100 or more to about five serious, dedicated candidates that align with your company culture.

Your time is too valuable to waste with people who do not belong within your organization. During the recruitment cycle, business owners hope that the next batch of applicants who enter is a good fit. However, instead of leaning your business on hope, you must create your victory as an entrepreneur. That starts with selecting the best people. Now, since you do not want to waste your time and ensure that every minute is valuable, I have a few tips that will help you avoid reading 1000's of CVs and save you time. Here it goes.

The first step in the recruitment process is only to entertain candidates who've successfully followed the video application strategy. You don't want to hire anyone who didn't put in the work of creating a video and sending it to you. Most people will be filtered out in this stage because they didn't follow your application instructions. The chances are, they didn't even read the full description. Instead, they were excited by the title and applied because their skillset was relevant to the job title. Don't read any CV that doesn't comply with the video strategy.

Applicants who don't read the full job description show a lack of drive and enthusiasm. In my not so humble opinion, it shows signs of laziness, which are not the kind of people you want working in your business if your goal is to grow your business successfully, which I am sure is every business owner's goal. Otherwise, why are you in business at all? That was a rhetorical question, folks!

After receiving several video applications, watch the applicant video; and only read the applicant's CV if you feel they align with your company's culture, value, vision, and goals. Can you see how much time this process will save you? Suppose you have previous experience with advertising a job within your company and have gone through the process of reading every CV that has applied to the job. In that case, you will appreciate how much time implementing this process will save you. I have just provided you with the secret ingredient to save yourself from reading 1000s of irrelevant CVs. You're welcome!

By following this process, not only will you save time from reading 1000s of irrelevant CV's but it will also save many hours in the interviewing stage, as you will only be interviewing the applicants who impress you with the video and appeal to you through the CVs. (We will discuss this process in further detail in the recruitment process section).

Hire Using the Talent Dynamics Profile Test

Roger James Hamilton introduced a sensational way of growing trust and creating flow within the organization. It can also be used in the recruitment phase. It is a leading tool used by more than 500,000 leaders globally. This test will help you scrutinize which of the eight profiles you fit the best, and conversely, which profiles do the person you are about to hire fit. This test works on the simple dynamics of understanding who you are and pursuing what comes to you naturally. The eight profiles are as follows:

1. **Creator**: People like Richard Branson who are naturally creative. These are the people who do not want to mess around with the specifics. Therefore, they will give you great ideas, but you need to find people who execute them.

2. **Star**: People like Oprah Winfrey could shine like a star and publicize your brand in a way that builds trust and authority in the eyes of its customers, employees, and stakeholders.

3. **Supporter**: People like Meg Whitman lead the team from the front and always keep people above others.

4. **Dealmaker**: People like Donald Trump who are excellent in negotiations. These people will get you the best deals every single time. Pay them well!

5. **Trader**: People like George Soros will give you the right advice and execution at the right time and take your business to the next level.

6. **Accumulator**: Great people like Warren Buffet and Charlie Munger might appear slow in the race but will always end up winning.

7. **Lord**: People like Angela Merkel who spend extra time giving all their attention to details. You need them, and they will save you more time than you could count. The clause in the fine print buried under the stack of contracts? They will find it and rescue you!

8. **Mechanic**: People like Mark Zukerberg always go above and beyond to perfect the systems other people could use, making their efforts easier and helping your business scale swiftly.

You need all the eight profiles in your business for it to become successful. The question is, at what stage are you willing to surface the true profile of a candidate? Or yours. In the very beginning! The sooner you know which piece falls where, the quicker your vision will come to life. According to the Talent Dynamics company, "talent Dynamics is different in that it provides an intuitive structure, practical strategies, modern role models and a link back to the roots of profiling 5,000 years ago."

You may be wondering, if there are many personality tests out there, then why am I encouraging you to go for this one? It's because I've been using it in my business to discern the exact personality of my employees and have first-hand experience of the benefits of using this test within my recruitment process. For complete honesty, I am an affiliate partner. However, you can go directly to their website if you prefer, or you can use the link provided in the book (giving me a small percentage of the total amount spent). However, I am sharing it with my experience because it works efficiently every time. Let me give you the five benefits of using this system:

1. **Builds Trust**: This system opens up your horizons and highlights a formula especially for you to build trust with role models.
2. **Timeless**: Regardless of the time and era, this test will show how your strength synchronizes with time.

3. **Intuitive and easy**: Unlike most personality tests, talent dynamics is easily explained once you know all the eight profiles and how they relate to each other.

4. **Increases your flow**: Your flow is the thing you like to do. It identifies it and helps you to grow it.

5. **Links to your spirit**: It links to your team spirit and enables you to understand your mission and purpose.

Scaling Up Simplified

SCAN THE CODE NOW

We partnered with Talent Dynamics to bring you the best of both worlds. Take out your phone and scan the above QR code. This test is based on the Chinese I Ching of 5 elements. The test assesses your productivity, personality, strength, values, and behaviors; therefore, it assigns you the profile you belong to – unlocking your natural flow using this strategy. You can only activate your flow with the help of people and tasks you surround yourself with. Make your qualified candidates take the test, and you will know in which position they belong. It might be too late if you delay taking the test. Go ahead, your entire team needs it.

CREATING A RECRUITMENT SYSTEM

I will provide you with straightforward steps to create a robust recruitment system that you or your hiring team could utilize to recruit the best fit. As previously mentioned, you should manage this entire section in your default diary. Follow it in order:

1. Create the job description.
2. Create a budget for advertising.
3. If you don't already have a dedicated email address for recruitment only, create one.
4. Post your ad on many recruitment advertising platforms and your website.
5. Request your marketing team to promote the job description via your company's social media sites.
6. Schedule time in your default diary to watch the videos of applicants who've applied for the role. As discussed in the default diary section, you should already have time scheduled for recruitment in your diary, as recruitment should be one of your top tasks in the scaling-up process.
7. Read the CV of the successful video applicants.
8. Schedule a call via email with the qualified applicants. Schedule the time in your default diary. Therefore,

provide timings to the selected candidates that work best for you. People need to fall into your schedule if they are serious about working with you. Add the scheduled calls, time, mobile number, and candidate's name to your calendar (default diary); also, add this information to your CRM system or create a new spreadsheet to keep track of all your interviews. Follow this method when scheduling every interview stage (your assistant should manage this section because, by this stage, they will be able to access your default diary to see where you have available slots for recruitment). During the phone call, explain all the steps required to get successfully recruited for the role so that the applicants are fully prepared if they advance to the next stage.

9. Send an unsuccessful email to the applicants who did not pass the video application. Remember, the successful candidates will be based on whether they align with your company culture and vision at this stage. Thank the applicants who did not pass. Always leave a good taste – it helps with your reputation. All applicants who took the time to follow this process should be shown appreciation for their time. You never know who they might talk to in the future or if they might be suited for your company at a later stage. Always show gratitude to the applicants who have dedicated time to your company in any form.

10. Connect with the successful candidate via a telephone call in the confirmed time slot and ask questions that will further establish if they are suited to the company culture. Also, get a vibe of how you feel about them. The call interview stage should be more personal to get to know the candidate better rather than focusing on their skillset.

11. If they pass the telephonic interview, you can email the successful candidates to invite them for the second stage interview via a video call. Zoom or Skype are great platforms to use for this video call. Send all applicants a link to the interview and instructions on using the platform of your choice to avoid confusion before the interview to avoid wasting time. You can create a document that can be copied and pasted with each applicant to save you even more time. Just replace the candidate's name, date and time of the interview, and link to the interview.

During the video interview stage, you will better understand the applicants' character, why they are looking for a new role, etc. Don't get too technical during this stage. Pay attention to how they present themselves; whether they made an actual effort and don't look like they just got out of bed for the video interview. Also, pay attention to their body language and whether they prepared questions for the interview (candidates who have prepared questions for the interview demonstrate that they have concluded comprehensive research about you and your business, representing enthusiasm for the role. It goes without saying; you only want to hire someone genuinely excited to work for your company). It's advised to record and store all video interviews with the candidate's permission.

12. Invite the successful candidates from the video interview stage for the 3rd and final interview in person. However, if this is a remote working role and cannot be attended in person, invite them for the last interview via video call again. During the 3rd interview stage, you will dive into their skill set to assess whether their skills are suited to the role or will require additional training. Where applicable, it is recommended to invite the department manager to attend the final round of interviews to have a second opinion on the applicants. Once completing the final interview, the qualified applicants will move on to the next stage of the recruitment process. It is suitable to approve more than one applicant from the last round of interviews to move on to the next step of the application.

13. During this step of the process, request that the successful candidates perform a skill test related to the role they have applied for. For example, if it is an admin-

related role, they need to have excellent attention to detail. Then, create a task that will demonstrate this skill.

14. Finally, select the candidate who aligns best with your company culture and performs the best during the test. But remember the general rule that "skills can be taught but attitude, positivity, and determination can't."

15. A small investment is required in this section, but it is highly recommended to add to your recruitment budget. In addition, the candidate who passed the skill test should be requested to take on the talent dynamic test to ensure they will flow well within your team.

16. The final step of the recruitment process would be making a job offer to the selected candidate; creating an offer letter and employment contract for them. Ensure that the offer letter and contract state the working hours, salary, bonuses, probation period, etc.

This entire recruitment process may seem lengthy, but in reality, it will save you more time and prevent a high staff turnover. But, more importantly, this process will extract the diamonds resulting in a robust team and successful business.

QUESTIONS TO ASK DURING INTERVIEW STAGES

I can understand if you are feeling overwhelmed in any way. So, let me break it down to you even further and spoon-feed you all the questions and ideas for every stage. Would that simplify your process? I bet it will.

Stage 1: The first phone call

These are culture fit and personality-based questions; you should create questions that align with the company culture you are trying to create. For example, if you are trying to create a fun, playful, and inclusive culture, ask fun and surprising questions. Such as:

- What do you do for fun?
- What is your biggest personal goal? (This question will demonstrate how determined the candidate is, showing that they put some thought into planning their life).
- What is your favorite movie or theatre production, and why?
- What would your previous manager say about you?
- Are you still friends with any previous colleagues from your previous roles?
- Ask a question related to your website to establish whether they viewed it.
- What is our company's vision statement?
- What does a thriving company culture look like to you?
- How do you think this role will help you develop?

- If you could have one superpower, what would it be and why? (This question will show quite a lot about their personality, how caring they are, etc.).

Stage 2: Video interview

Ask further questions to get a feel of their character and why they are looking to change companies. Don't get too technical yet; leave the skill-based questions for the last interview.

- How do you respond to criticism?
- If you do not get this position, what will be your next career move?
- Is there a time you exceeded people's expectations? If yes, describe it
- What does your decision-making process look like?
- When was the last time you took a risk professionally?
- How do you stay organized?
- Why did you choose to apply here?
- How do you prefer to communicate with coworkers?
- What motivates you to do your best work?
- How would you describe your group of friends?
- What books, blogs, and websites do you read in your free time?

Stage 3: In-person or second video interview. Get technical!

During this stage, ask them questions related to their CV experience, skill sets, expertise, etc. This section will be based on the role you are hiring for, but I have provided a few question samples to set you on the right track.

- Can you discuss a time where you had to manage your team through a difficult situation?
- How do you prioritize your tasks when you have multiple deadlines to meet?
- What is the most significant problem you solved in the workplace?
- How do you explain new topics to co-workers who are unfamiliar with them?
- Describe a situation where the results went against your expectations. How did you adapt to this change?
- What are your actions if employees disagree with your decision?
- Name three of your most important considerations when working for an employer.
- Highlight a situation where you had to decide without managerial supervision. What did you do to approach this situation, and who else did you speak with?
- When have you performed a task without pre-existing experience?
- Explain your most significant failure at work. How and what did you learn from this experience?

- Ask questions related to their CV to ensure they have not just copied and pasted their CVs from job descriptions.

Of course, you are not confined to asking these questions only, but they provide you with a general idea.

CAREERS PAGE

A career page or site is a subsection of your website that showcases your brand and recent job openings. It can be one landing page, a subdomain, or a hybrid. The bottom line is, your business must have a careers page. It should have only one purpose: to introduce yourself to the job seekers and project your values, why your employees love working there, and what benefit they hold? The content you display on this page is your first expression for your potential employees. They will assess it thoroughly and decide whether they want to apply or not. Use it as a branding tool and a way to receive applicants who would be a great asset to your company.

There are multiple benefits of having a careers page. Let's go through it one by one:

1. A company with a vision needs a story that could entice employees and customers. Unfortunately, most people do not leverage this segment and thus remain untapped for years. The careers page enables you to tell your story

to potential candidates. How did you start, the obstacles you faced, and more – make a connection.

2. It enhances your organic traffic. For example, most job seekers search for the term "industry + careers" or "company + career," what do you think your odds are to show up on the first page? It's much higher with a careers page.

3. It expresses your feelings. The story you tell will create a special place in the people's hearts who stumble upon your website. You will instantly stand out from all the other businesses who didn't tell their story – pretty cool, isn't it?

4. A careers page reduces your hiring cost and time because it will organically pull applicants in from the careers page. In addition, it will reduce your advertising cost, and candidates will be pre-qualified from the career page.

5. You can easily track visitors who land on your webpage and who move on without taking any action. Then, you can retarget and remind them about your business through Facebook, Instagram, or google ads by using target marketing (retargeting will be discussed in further detail in chapter 8).

Invest in creating a great careers page today because it will not only save you time and money; it will build your reputation and increase your brand value. In addition, you will get a great response from your potential employees. However, that can only be achieved when you take care of a few things. First, never tell two conflicting stories with the same brand. Your story should be consistent on your website and across all social media platforms. Second, be creative and utilize different media to narrate your story.

People consume content in multiple ways; some watch videos, some like to read, and others only need to see a picture. Your job is to be everywhere and create your brand across all media – be very cautious of what you show to your audience and how you show it. There might be perspective issues, so be prepared and evaluate before publishing to the whole world.

Third, clearly explain who you are, what you stand for, and what you believe in, which will unify your message and help you focus on the singular mission. Fourth, have the employee avatar in your mind while constructing a careers page. You aren't marketing to everyone. You need people who align with your culture and values; therefore, jot down the personality of the created content accordingly. People who do not fit within your parameters could pass on. Lastly, walk the talk. It's not enough to just make bold promises; you should be able to keep them and show people that you live the words you speak. Not committing to your words might result in the employees abandoning your company. If you promise a specific work-life to your employees, give it to them when they get onboard.

IMPORTANCE OF KPIs

A key Performance indicator or KPI is a measurement system that showcases a company's performance over time. It helps you evaluate the strategic, financial, and operational progress of your company. This data will enable you to make better decisions regarding your revenue, profits, and investments. You can keep track of all the critical numbers, and it is easy to measure.

KPIs will measure your success and target the achieving ability of your company. It will also show your position with your competition. All the financial questions about liquidity, expenses, cash flow; will be answered here. You can use KPIs to target your customers and keep track of their efficiency, satisfaction, and retention. The other use is with a specific aim in mind to measure a goal and monitor performance. Your long-term success depends on utilizing the KPIs to optimize various business attributes and setting your business up for long-term success.

Creating Efficient KPIs For Your Company

KPIs aren't just performance indicators; they also display each employee's role in the organization. Knowing which employee is responsible for doing what could save you a lot of hassle in the future. It also defines your desired outcome, the progress towards that outcome, and the person who influences it. The SMART acronym we discussed in the goals chapter is also very useful in the KPI. Here is how it works:

- Having a **specific** aim and a route paved to reach it
- The goal you set should be **measurable**
- Setting an **attainable** goal
- Is the set goal **relevant** to the overall company?
- In what **time frame** are you looking to achieve that goal?

I cannot stress how vital it is to reassure the goal and the path you are walking on by re-evaluating your business strategy. If you find an even more straightforward approach, take that. Of course, your company goals will vary as well. At the end of the year, if you achieved beyond your set company goal, then ask yourself whether the goal was too low or whether your company performed admirably. Conversely, if your company didn't reach the set goals, ask yourself whether the goal was too difficult or the problem was in the systems and team, and what changes could make you reach your goal the next time?

Let's proceed with the development part. Every KPI is unique to each business as they face different problems. Your KPI should help you achieve your goals and signify the role of each. To create a KPI, you need the following five things:

1. Specific goal to achieve
2. Progress measuring indicator
3. Success and failure criteria
4. Steps to take when you run off-track
5. Steps to take when you couldn't achieve your goals

Earlier, people had to make a KPI on a spreadsheet, which was time-consuming and prone to error. Lucky for you, today we have many free and paid software that will provide you with beautiful layouts of the company with every key data in it. For instance, if you wish to create a KPI for your marketing team, they will contain the following segments:

- Traffic information, where people are coming from, and how long they are staying on your website
- Your search history means the searches people made to reach you on the internet
- List of pages where most of your audience first landed
- The leads you obtained through the landing page

- Number of actions taken on your page, for example, adding products to cart, checking out, payment, and success
- The reviews and ratings of the product or service on the internet through various sources
- How many people left your website, and why?
- Your SEO and ads (Google) performance
- and more...

You can use software like Eloomi, Gecko board, smart sheet, Cyfe, scoreboard, Sisense, GoodData, etc. Your KPIs must be shared with everyone in the company, whether employees, shareholders or other management members. Everyone must know the roles of each person, the set goals, and the way to follow the performance. When done, you need to make sure that you review the KPI periodically and update it with time.

PROBATION PERIOD AND INDUCTION TRAINING

According to a survey from Opinion matters, 18% of the recruits fail probation. That's a massive chunk of your team. Probation is the trial period for your recruits; it can last from 3-12 months. You do not want to break apart your team because you didn't take an additional step to verify your recruit. Most people are great in the interview, on resumes, but you need real-life results. They should meet the KPIs, learn to follow your system, adapt to your company culture, get along as a team member and prove their worth. That's the purpose of the probation period – it is a safety step for your business. Business doesn't rely on your opinions; it depends on the facts and figures. So, begin the recruitment by distrusting the new staff member. To have a great successful business, you must allow staff to prove trustworthy and an asset to the company.

I highly recommend you pay the recruit less during the probation period and when they pass with flying colors, then start their actual salary. You should introduce this in the interview process and get their approval in writing, which may be when most people put their foot down and bow out. Still, you will also receive committed and dedicated people using this filter system. Keep it between 20% to 50% of their actual salary as far as the probation pay goes. Test them for a quarter, and examine if they meet the KPIs. You can then increase their income to the actual salary once passing the probation period.

For probation to work successfully and for your new member to prove their worth, you need to meet them halfway and provide full training within their role. No one will be able to perform to their best ability if full training is not provided. All training should be scheduled, tracked, checklists, and signed off. New recruits should be provided with a welcome pack and training material for their coaching session. Training should be delivered in two forms.

Form #1: Induction training

Induction training is all about the company, how everything works, who your clients are, the value system, the goals and vision, form of communication with clients, branding, team members, company history with the purpose, the software used, etc. It is recommended that the induction last roughly a day, depending on how big your organization is. A welcome or induction pack should be provided with the induction training with all the information regarding the induction.

Form #2: Actual role training

It is crucial to train all new team members on how to perform their role within your organization, use all the software, store all documentation, and how the systems and processes work within the role. By the end of the training, a new team member should feel confident to start their new role with minimal oversight. This training element will differ depending on the position and business, but a good duration is roughly 1 to 2 weeks of training. All your systems and processes must be ready for each new role, which can be used as guidelines once the training is completed so that the recruit understands precisely what is required of them in their role. Providing proper training leaves very little room for errors and excuses.

Meetings During the Probation Period

To measure the recruit's success within the probation period, regular performance meetings should be held for you and the new starter to understand how they are performing within the role. If there is an element of the role they are struggling with or might need extra guidance and training; performance meetings will help the new starter to successfully integrate into the new position and also allow you as the business owner or manager of the department to establish whether the new starter is a good fit for the company.

It is best to plan and schedule meetings in advance when the new team member joins the team to be aware of the meeting dates in advance to prepare. If you have provided full training, held constructive feedback meetings, and focused on the areas the new starter might lack, and the recruit is still not fully integrated by the end of the probation period, they might not be suited for the role and company. It's advised to end the contract at this point or offer an additional month of probation if you are under the impression they will do well after being provided with an extra month of training. Use your best judgment.

TEAM MEETINGS

One of the main reasons businesses don't explode with success is that they aren't communicating with employees. People walk in, do the assigned tasks, and return home as soon as the evening bell rings. The management has lost credibility, and the chart is slamming downwards rather than upwards. I don't want your company to be amongst these unsuccessful organizations. Team meetings are the way to end these horrors. You need to arrange team meetings every week. Block out all external noise for a couple of hours and sit down with your employees to evaluate them and your company's status.

Set the agenda upfront, so that the team is fully prepared. Meetings should be used to improve your progress regarding your quarterly or yearly goals. Discuss the matters that hold the top priority. Depending on your culture, you can turn these meetings into short informative time slots or a bit fun and playful, allowing your employees to connect.

At the start of the Scaling Up process, your team will be smaller; therefore, the entire team could attend the meetings. However, when you have multiple departments, ensure the meetings occur within each department so that your staff's time isn't wasted. Keep it short and meaningful. Evaluate where your company stands at the meeting time and what is required to reach your quarterly goals.

If you're wondering what to discuss in the meetings as most business owners do, then let me help you with that as well. First you can evaluate the statistics of each member. Let them projec their weekly accomplishments on a simple line graph, making it easier for everyone to see if the line is going up or down. If the chart is positive, then you have nothing to worry about; ask them what they will be doing to keep it growing, though. Conversely, if the graph is declining or negative, ask them why it is and their plans to turn it into a positive chart.

The science behind it is, nobody wants to sit in a meeting with a negative graph. They will feel embarrassed and do everything in their power to bring in a positive result – good news for your company, isn't it?

The second thing you can cover in the meeting is targets. Managers will describe the handed targets for the team and whether they are met or not, the reasoning, and more. The third topic could be the problem faced during the week and the solutions that they came up with. If there are still unsolved matters, you can brainstorm to find a solution collectively. Finally, you can also ask for the victories they've accomplished during the week. People need recognition and appreciation; it would make their day if you could reward or simply appreciate them during the meeting. It will also spark a positive interest within every one of them to do more and win more. Isn't that a healthy competition? I think so too!

You can even start with a review of your goals. It is natural to end the meeting with goals, but we've seen that starting with them helps you frame the performance review of the goals. Next, provide goals to each employee and also set them up to improve. Everyone has different motivations; some need money, some need development, some need appreciation, and some need it all. Understanding each employee's priority motivator will help you inspire them and make the later discussion about the improvement more fruitful.

Furthermore, you should be aware of the perspective the employee holds. Everybody has a level at which they operate, so ask them their definition of high performance. For example, you may think that sending around 80 emails a day means high performance, but it could be 50, according to them. Know the gap, and do not judge them based on your perspective.

While discussing the accomplishments, explain why it is essential for the business so that when talking about their downfall or weaknesses, they understand the consequences for not accomplishing their goals. Then, provide them a chance to come up with great ideas to improve themselves and their productivity etiquette. All meetings should be tracked and recorded for future references. For example, you can set up the meeting minutes and begin the next one by reviewing the minutes of the previous meeting. Following this method make it easier to keep track of everything and eliminates confusion and misunderstandings.

This chapter was a longer one for a reason. In business, employees are the key players. Employees make your dream a reality. I needed to walk you through the process so that you can save your time, build a powerful team, and witness exponential growth. When all the pieces fall into place, it is time for you to discard your role from the business. A successful business can run without you; therefore, the next chapter will teach you systemization. You can take your time in this chapter and re-read it if necessary. Then, when you're ready, let's proceed.

CHAPTER SIX

KEY TO RUNNING A BUSINESS WITHOUT YOU

"Investing in management means building communication systems, business processes, feedback, and routines that let you scale the business and team as efficiently as possible."

– Fred Wilson

E ver heard the quote "running around like a headless chicken?" Do you feel like that in your business? I can assume that you are experiencing this in your company because you don't have systems and processes in place for your team to follow, so they revert to you for every decision that needs to be made, every mistake that occurs, and hence you feel like you're running around like a headless chicken; constantly putting out fires. Again, this is because systems and processes have a significant role in building a company.

They serve as an essential building block that supports the growth of your business. It makes the process seamless and spreads happiness among the employees. One of the main reasons you should invest in systems and processes is to gain accuracy, efficiency and remove yourself from the business – that is the ultimate key. This chapter is designed to teach you what systems and processes are, how to create them, and how to run a business without you. One of the most significant challenges business owners like you face is not being able to delegate effectively. Not knowing how to let go will always keep you busy IN the business and rip you off from the blessing of working ON the business. It impedes business growth and affects productivity in the workplace.

We, humans, have 35000 thoughts each day, and we make a decision based on it. Imagine if you have only ten employees; that's 350,000 thoughts roaming around in your company. If you have more employees, then you can do the math. With so much energy being wasted behind thought processing, what are the chances of people making the right decision every time? Great leaders recommend making only 3-5 decisions per day because they know that whatever comes after could be indecision.

After knowing that there is so much room for indecision, do you want to leave your business at the mercy of the people with chaos in their minds? I certainly don't. Even if you have skilled employees, the possibility of each having genius ideas is only 5 out of 35,000; but there will be thousands of other decisions that could go horribly wrong. Currently, if you feel that your business is a mess and nothing is going right, again, you probably don't have any systems or processes in place that people could follow. Now, how do you know if your business is self-sufficient? Here are two exclusive tickets to Hawaii for a five nights trip to the most luxurious hotel available. Enjoy yourself; send some pictures while you're at it. What? Can't you go? You are too scared of what will happen to your business in your absence? That is an indication of poor business management, which is a recipe for disaster and could be the reason behind many wrong decisions until there is no business left to work on.

Systems and businesses are essential to business growth. If there is no verified system to recruit an employee, run your daily activities, and market your product, there is literally no room for scaling the business. As a result, growth will be difficult, if not wholly impossible. Your business needs to have the systems and processes for every position in your business, from sales and management to recruiting and training.

I am not saying to build rigorous methods for people to follow like robots; the aim isn't to kill their creativity. However, you should create some specific foundational guidelines for each role to follow, ensuring that a consistent result is gained without significant issues or errors. It also becomes easier to replace a position. We all know what a nightmare it is when one of your employees leaves your company, especially after working together for years. The business gets dependent on them and you; hence, to avoid that, you need systems that could turn any skillful recruit to consistently produce the same number of results. That way, you don't have to take the plunge and roll up your sleeves, limiting your growth even more.

Take a look at McDonalds, Starbucks, KFC, or any of the franchises; no matter which country you're from or which store you walk in, you will get the same taste every time. On top of that, they hire and fire at will. Therefore, anybody could join McDonalds, pass their training program, and start flipping burgers with absolute accuracy. Why do you think that is? The founders and creators of McDonalds aren't even alive right now, and the business is still making money left and right.

Simply put, they have specific systems and processes in place that enable them to produce the same tasty meal, train people, and run smoothly without a constant need to check upon. The average age of a McDonald's manager is around 24 years old. They can employ such young managers and have businesses worldwide because they have solid systems that their employees can follow. I believe that a business that couldn't be replicated and scaled up without you, isn't a business; it's a job. *"Spend time upfront to invest in systems and processes to make long-term growth sustainable."* – Jeff Platt.

Systems save you time, money, and a lot of hassle. It is a se of processes, people, and technologies integrated to get the job done. The way you install systems is that every time you are faced with a problem, your brain should instantly discern ideas to solve it not temporarily but permanently. Ask yourself: "What can I do now that will make this problem go away forever?" Once you find a rigid solution, automate it and ensure it's developed into the best version. There are technologies that can be utilized to assist in running your business efficiently—for example, accounting software, CRM systems, sales funnels, etc. The system's role within a company is to inform us who needs to manage these interfaces and who needs to be accountable, which then becomes a set of processes, people, technologies, and interfaces.

Furthermore, it also dictates how they communicate with other interfaces within your business. You need both systems and processes to succeed in your business – systems improve efficiency while processes enhance effectiveness. You can systemize your finance, marketing, sales inductions, operations, and pretty much everything. Then, all you need to do is plant people to maintain those systems.

Conversely, a process is a set of steps required to fulfill a task repeatedly. A series of concrete sequential steps magnify effectiveness and reduce time when duplicated over and over. A task that you or your team are performing frequently, should be formulated into a process. However, the process should be thoroughly proofed, meaning, following the process should guarantee the results. For example, suppose your sales team arranges a meeting with your clients. In that case, they may send an email with the slots available to book a date; clients will choose the slot and respond to reserve their slot, and your team will send your client a confirmation message regarding the meeting, and then remind them about the meeting in advance, for example, three days before, one day before, an hour before, and so forth.

The example mentioned above will be the process; you know it works, and you've logged it in. If you think that you could optimize this process to gain more effectiveness, like instead of sending reminder emails, people are more active and responsive to SMS or slack messages; incorporate that instead. Therefore, when they're inquiring how to schedule a meeting, nobody from the sales team has to waste time explaining; just hand them the log, and you're good. Isn't it effective? Write steps down and turn them into a process, which is how you can easily measure quality and consistency.

PROCESSES YOUR BUSINESS NEEDS

There could be hundreds of businesses out there similar to yours; therefore, to stand out from the crowd, the only point of difference is the way you execute and deliver the promise. Think what Domino's did, when they were swamped with competitors who were catching up on the pizza making business, they geared up by introducing a new scheme called "guaranteed 30-minute delivery or free pizza". This slight twist gave them an upper hand. People were buying pizza from them like crazy, and Domino's came out victorious. After monitoring and measuring your processes, you can optimize them to find effective solutions to carry out the tasks at hand and achieve your company goals. You should create procedures for tasks that will repeat in each role and department. Think of how the role or task could be performed to the best of its ability, without involvement from you, and create a simple process duplicating the results.

If you are still baffled by which task to create systems and procedures for, here are a few examples to focus on:

1. **Customer assimilation**: This is a solid process where you will imprint your first expression upon your customers, show them what you're capable of, excite them by under-promising, and knock their socks off with over-delivering – make them proud of their decision to engage with your company. Set a grateful screen, some free but valuable stuff to be downloaded via email, and an introductory call from an executive or anything that will make you stand out and entice them to remain loyal customers. It is one of the most critical processes, so let everybody in your team know its importance and prioritize it.

2. **Customer interfacing:** This is the process where you define the line of communication with your current customer base. It will enable you to find opportunities for upselling them additional products and services or extend the services you're currently providing. Either way, it will be a great addition to your existing revenue.

3. **Customer retraction:** Even though the customers retract their engagement with your company, there should still be a pleasant experience that leaves them with a sweet taste of your company. The smoother the process is, the more likely you are to get a referral. Nevertheless, make an effort to collect their exact reason for leaving your business and ensure that the same issues don't reoccur with your future clients.

4. **Budgets**: Your budgets and how you compile them are of great importance. New business owners are always at risk of running out of cash. Therefore, to keep track of your expenditure and run your business smoothly, you need a process for budgets.

5. **Annual accounting**: Accounting may not be the most attractive side of your business, but it is one of the most important. Establish a process to calculate your annual revenue and manage accounts for the financial year. This will keep your taxes in check and thus provide a robust system to operate with accuracy and peace of mind. (To be explained in detail in chapter 7).

6. **Remuneration**: Taking care of your employees is a crucial segment of your job. Employees should be paid well and on time. Make it dynamic so that any deductions or bonuses can be arranged without any confusion.

7. **Tax reduction:** Businesses could save a lot of money in taxes if they do it right. Having a definite process to submit paperwork and preparing well could help you regain the money owed to you.

8. **Employee Grievance:** In the workplace, sometimes there can be disputes and arguments. It may lead to grievance; therefore, your business system needs to have a specific process in place to address any grievance that comes from an employee; try to investigate the problem's validation (whether it really happened or not), listen to the whole story from both sides, and then appeal for fair justice. You may not have to use it very often, but in any case, it is great to have something – you do not want your culture to fall apart because of this.

9. **Employee holidays:** You may have specific rules for accepting holiday requests from employees; just like every company does. However, do you have a process in place to grant holidays over the agreed terms? For example, there could be an emergency, and the employee might ask you for a couple of days off. During this time, examine the place they are coming from and have a process that manages everything in their absence. There

should be a calendar that depicts how many people are away at any given time.

10. **Employee assimilation**: Businesses underestimate their employee onboarding process. It ensures how you make your recruit feel on the first day and how they get along. Their retention period will showcase how well you executed this task – it's a gesture to demonstrate how much you care as a company.

11. **Employee offboarding:** Similar to customers, your adored employees also deserve a proper farewell to encourage positive reviews and referrals. There could be many reasons for them to leave the company; it's not always your fault. Arrange a farewell for them, bring a cake, talk about their journey and how they got along, say good things about them, and more. They will never forget your company.

12. **Performance review**: It should be a transparent metric that enables your employees to showcase their capabilities. This will help them to work harder and rank up their performances. You should praise them when they hit their goals or exceed your expectations. In addition, clarify the process, which will exhibit what needs to be done to improve if someone isn't performing well. Finally, reward them for their work, and suddenly you will have an army trying to make you rich.

13. **Pre-recruitment**: There is a pool of potential not yet hired candidates waiting to join your company. It is essential that you communicate the entire process of getting hired and choose the candidate who meets all the requisites to give them a positive experience even if they are not selected for further rounds.

14. **Key partnerships:** One of the best ways to grow your business is to build connections with companies that complements your business but are not in competition. Don't try to be a lone wolf. For example, architecture firms can partner up with established interior decorators or individuals and help each other with potential leads. Join up with them and grow together. This way, you can complement each other's strengths and overcome weaknesses to establish a firm business that stays forever in the minds of its consumers. Have a process to choose partners that fit perfectly with your culture and values. The question is not only about money, its ethics, morals, reputation, and more.

15. **Review:** Processes cannot stay stagnant forever. You will have to revisit and improve them regularly to ensure compliance, efficiency, and effectiveness.

16. **Procurement**: Every business needs software and other tools to work efficiently. Set up a documenting process for purchasing goods and services that help you to run your business smoothly and achieve the required

result. For example, your marketing team may need software for creating beautiful, engaging videos. Most of them work on the subscription model.

17. **Business strategy**: A business without a definite plan is doomed to fail. You make strategic decisions based on your core values and vision. Build a process to revise your targets and goals, track your progress, and how to maneuver your growth towards success.

18. **Competitor scrutinization:** It is said to keep your enemies closer than your friends. You need to know what your competitors are up to and what you can do to beat them and gain the upper hand. Have a process that helps your marketing team to conduct thorough research on your rivals.

19. **Customer acquisition:** Businesses use different ways to acquire customers. It all boils down to where your ideal customers hang out and targeting them there. You can use social media platforms, sales calls, and more. Knowing more about your customers, their preferences, and what excites them is crucial to lead the market. Have a detailed step-by-step procedure regarding customer acquisition and make sure your team follows it and acquires as many customers as possible – the more, the merrier.

20. **Promotion:** No business can scale without publicity. You must get your name out there, make a noise that will

be heard. Your product needs attention, and the only way to do that, is to have a dedicated process and team to promote and publicize the brand and what you stand for – conduct events, advertise, tv shows, or whatever you can to get noticed. First, however, conduct excellent research about your audience and then go full force to gain customers.

USING CHECKLISTS

After discussing and creating systems and processes, you need to narrow everything down to a checklist that your team could use as a guideline while following the procedure. They can then have the satisfaction of checking things off from the list and getting approved by the manager to ensure every step has been followed to fulfill the task successfully. We get a tremendous level of fulfillment when we complete a task and then cross it off from the list. Employees will work harder to cross off every task, which is a plus point of having a checklist. Of course, this is not the whole reason why you should utilize a checklist. It also secures the success of repeated tasks, avoiding any form of errors or, at the very least, limiting them to the minimum.

As a business owner, you have already committed the mistakes, which were then created into a process of what not to do and formulated into a checklist. If the employee still makes the same mistake, they were either not given the training well or are lazy and not following the processes and checklists. It is advisable that employees only start using their "own" intuition once they are extremely comfortable within the role and can suggest various ways to improve the current processes. Before implementing any procedures, a meeting should be conducted with the department manager and signed off.

A checklist is a simple tool that helps you to prevent these mistakes from ever happening again. It is simply a standardized list of the required steps developed for a repetitive task or processes. If this doesn't entice you, then here are seven benefits of using a checklist:

1. It helps you to be more organized by providing easy-to-follow steps, causing effective results. A to-do list is a special form of a checklist that allows you to manage all your tasks in one place quickly. You can schedule activities and not let anything come your way.

2. Checklists inspire the employees and you to get the job done. When you cross off the first task, you are then motivated to cross off the second and third until you are successfully sitting with a crossed-out sheet – it's simply a positive impact of accomplishing one task after another.

3. It enhances your productivity. Since repeated tasks are taken care of easily, the process will have fewer errors. A

a result, you will have more time left in your day to take on more work if you want to accomplish more, or you could go home to your family with a smile and a sense of accomplishment in your heart. Bryan Tracy said, "*The checklist is one of the most high-powered productivity tools ever discovered.*"

4. It magnifies your creativity. Checklists allow you to master the redundant tasks, which leaves more room for thinking clearly and being creative. In addition, it reduces stress, and thus you have energy stored to utilize on gaining creative ways to accomplish a task or a new way to scale your business – I leave it up to you!

5. It gives you peace of mind while delegating the tasks. Business owners are reluctant to delegate because they are concerned about the completion and quality, well no more! Having a specific checklist for the task will ensure completion while following the process. You can now delegate your tasks and feel good about them.

6. It intensifies your effectiveness regarding the tasks. Showcasing the superiority in the market by providing absolute customer service, you will gain more respect in the eyes of your customers. It can then create a snowball effect of references and word of mouth.

7. Checklists have the power to save many lives. I am not exaggerating. When a surgical team implemented using a checklist to conduct an operation, the death rate since

then has come down by 40%. There was another incident in World War 2 where an aviator flight crashed. After that, pilots were told to use a checklist before taking off, and they still use it today.

I always say that if you want to do something repeatedly without any errors, use a checklist.

LEADERSHIP AND DELEGATION

A system without a brilliant driver is as good as having no system at all. Leadership is the most crucial component of running a business. You can be the best technician, but are you the best leader your business has ever got? Ask yourself this question, and when you do, you will realize one of the key roles as a leader in mastering the art of delegation. No human is perfect, not even me. You can and should be exceptionally good at something, but not everything. Business is the game where you can bring in people to fill out roles you aren't good at. Do what you love and the tasks taking too much of your time due to lack of finesse, delegate it to someone who loves doing them. You can love your business like a baby without micromanaging every aspect of it. Didn't you know that? Well, now you do!

In every business, you need an operations manager that can drive the systems and processes you have in place, lead and motivate the team, and ensure that you are on track with you goals – as we discussed in chapter 5 about hiring according to your weak areas. If you are the visionary in your business (which most entrepreneurs are), you would probably struggle with the operations element of your business. You must hire someone within your establishment to ensure that your team is driven under your leadership.

I believe that most business owners aren't aware of the difference between management and leadership. They are two polar opposites. Management means supervising a group of people with systems and processes to achieve a specific goal. Conversely, leadership is the art of developing an ability to influence, inspire, and encourage people to contribute to the organization's greater good. These two words, "influence and inspiration," separate management from leadership – they both have equal authority. Apart from being a visionary, you can still be a great leader who inspires others to be the best version of themselves. Motivate the operations manager to confirm that everything in your business runs as planned to the best of its ability.

It's not for everyone, as most visionaries won't be very good at leading a team using the systems and processes. Moreover, they also find it challenging to delegate like a leader. If you don't delegate the tasks, you're average or bad at, you will always get an average or bad quality outcome. But, on the other hand, delegating effectively will help you get more things done in an accelerated time frame, enhance your team spirit, and you can focus on the tasks you're most passionate about or exclusively known to you. Therefore, I will give you five simple steps that will help you to master delegation.

Step 1: Deciding what to delegate

There are two types of tasks you need to delegate as a leader. The first type of task is the one that is not the most crucial but is still taking up a massive chunk of your time. This is the task you delegate to the less experienced people so that you save a lot of time while the task is still being completed by someone else. The second type of task is the one that is more important to the company, but you don't have the required expertise or finesse to get it done with top-notch quality. Therefore, you delegate it to someone who is an expert in that particular field. In both instances, you can satisfactorily focus on the tasks that only you can do or love, which is strategizing or envisioning how to take your business to the next level.

Step 2: Clarifying the expectations and processes

While giving up the tasks, you need to ensure that you make things clear to them. It shouldn't be that the person you're delegating the task to, wastes more time than you would on that task and gets nowhere. Therefore, you need to communicate about the task with your team, the required outcome, and the deadline. Moreover, give them the process to follow, which secures the successful completion, and a checklist to make your job easier and inspire them to work effectively.

When you choose a team member to delegate your task to, explain the purpose and why they are selected for the job. While carrying out the tasks, there might be numerous unforeseen circumstances, so clarify what authority they have to use their judgment and when they should approach you in decision-making. Establish some accountability upon the task; what are the things you will be asking for so that they are prepared upfront. Finally, if they have any questions, answer them. *"Delegating doesn't mean passing off work you don't enjoy, but letting your employees stretch their skills and judgment."* – Harvey Mackay.

Step 3: Empower your staff

Delegation isn't getting rid of tedious work. Instead, it allows your employees to show what they are capable of. Stretch them out of their comfort zones by giving them challenging tasks, but also let them make their own decisions in the process and hold themselves accountable. Empower your staff to be the best version of themselves. Groups can only thrive when every one of them is sold on the idea of adding value to the bigger picture by fulfilling the tasks handed down to them – when they are given an opportunity to shine and the power to make their best judgment. It's OK if they fail a couple of times initially, don't fire them for making mistakes, let them learn, and get better if they are willing to do so.

Step 4: Learn to let go

This is the problem I see with many managers and business owners; they do not want to give the task up. They think that they can do the task better than anyone else in the company when that is not the case in reality. Learn to embrace your limitations and let the tasks go to someone who could do it better and faster than you – if you don't, it's the biggest failure for you in the journey of becoming a successful entrepreneur. Nobody wants to work for a boss who thinks they are better than everyone and can't let things go. If they do, they will be around every second micro-managing each activity; they will try to immediately take over when they find one wrong step. So, do you want to be the boss who everybody hates?

Give others the chance to grow and shine; you are not to compete with your employees; you all are in the same team. Trust the people you're working with; you hired them yourself didn't you? They are here to make your life easier. If you keep thinking that people around you are idiots, they will be idiots, add no value, or they will leave your company and create a legacy elsewhere. It is stupidity to hire smart people and then tell them what to do, Steve Jobs said himself. You hire them so that they can do things better than you.

Step 5: Invest your time and reap greater rewards

Train your staff to deliver at the highest level every time; if they don't, it's a failure for you as a leader. If you are scared to delegate to them, you haven't trained them well to produce results. Uplift them to do more tasks and improve their skills so that you can delegate without a second thought. I don't know where it came from, but business owners and managers have a misguided approach towards delegation, as they think that it is faster if they don't waste time training others and simply do the work themselves. Do you see the fault in that statement? It's a short-term perspective that will surely save you a few minutes in the present but hurt your business in the long term. Why? Because instead of spending time as a visionary, you wasted time doing tasks that could be delegated to other people who were sitting around while you were running around like a headless chicken.

See the bigger picture and let everyone play a role in making it a reality. Don't intend to grab all the prestige for yourself; it's not a sign of a leader. Great leaders help others to be the best and then share their spotlight. The captain of the Indian cricket team showcases similar attributes. When the team wins, he sends his players to take part in the interview and grab all the attention; however, when the team loses, he shows up to face all the critics and haters himself – that's the kind of leader you want to be.

Think about what kind of message you are sending to your team. Show them trust, respect, and allow them the platform to perform. Spend that time with them. They might not get it perfectly the first time, but they will be better the third or fourth time, and by then, you will have people working at the same level as you are in completing a task – that's your end goal.

What Happens When You Don't Delegate?

The mere act of delegation is an essential skill for managers and business owners. However, there are certain risks involved for people who fail to delegate from an early stage. The first risk is that your performance will suffer. Doing everything yourself will exhaust you, and hence all the decisions you make will then backfire. You are not good at everything, and you will keep forgetting things when there are multiple tasks to take care of - you will be toxic for your own business.

Your personal life will suffer as well. That is the second risk. Always stressing out about all the tasks being carried out will leave you vulnerable and unable to find the perfect work-life balance. All you would think of is whether that process i followed, or that email has been sent, or one of the million othe things. The third risk is that you will never excel in anything. *The jack of all trades is the master of none*; the saying is famous for a reason. There is no way you will be the super expert in any field if you keep doing 100 things all at once. Multitasking is a myth; shatter it today! The greatest players, business owners, and experts have secured that place because they only pursued what they were great at. Forget what school taught you about leaving the things you can do for those you can't; that's a wrong perception. Business is an entirely different game.

You went out of your way to set up a process to hire the best people out there. They need to be challenged, they need to be trusted, and they need to be given a chance to prove their capabilities. *"Delegation requires the willingness to pay for short-term failures, to gain long term competency."* – Dave Ramsey. Only then will you have a high-performing team that inspires the world.

USING CRM TO DELEGATE EFFICIENTLY

A CRM is a system of processes that helps you to organize your delegation process. It will enable you to share your success with your team. Hence, it will draw out confidence within them, and you can focus on your core business. However, you do not want to just leave everything to them without even paying attention. That's when a CRM comes in. Online software will keep track of every activity happening in and around your business – you now have an amazing tool to monitor and control things without leaving your cabin. Here's how it can be used:

1. **Divide tasks efficiently**: CRM can be integrated into your systems, converting any emails you send into a task. Now, you can share calendar slots with your employees and plan everything upfront – it gives a fair chance to everybody.

2. **Follow up from anywhere:** There is a fine difference between micro-management and following up. You should avoid the first and do the latter. It keeps you in control and stress-free. Every time a task, meeting, or phone call is checked off, you can see it in the system and follow up to verify and gain details at any time.

3. **Monitor results in real-time:** We all know that it is challenging to keep track of everything that happens in your company at once, don't worry; the CRM got you covered. You can now get a comprehensive statistical analysis of all the tasks. It's easy to gain insights, reduces your work, and let you sleep better knowing everything is running well.

4. **Centralize your information:** You shouldn't be the only important contact for all information. It's a massive downfall for your business. Using CRM, you can create a centralized system to store information for people to access. It's easier when accessed through mobile devices

5. **Software for growth**: CRM is one of the tools that is designed to benefit your business. There are many more tools readily available in the market can boost your productivity by establishing effective systems.

To exhibit how much my team and I care about CRM systems to bring efficiency to the workplace, we partnered with one of the best systems available for you today. It's called Monday.com; it brings efficient workflows into your business and enables you to manage every aspect of your business from one single destination. I'll place a QR code below, and all you have to do is use your phone to scan it, and you will be directed to their portal, where you can sign up and initiate the process. So do not hold back, my friend, as this single step is going to change the way you used to operate forever. Here's the special code only for you!

SCAN THE CODE NOW

159

All your systems and processes should be stored on a cloud device such as Google Drive. Everything should be very well organized with a seamless flow so that your team can access the needed information without any effort or confusion. Each department and team member should have access to the relevant drive folder. When a new team member joins, they can have access to this folder as well. You can also create a drive folder for each team member when they join your team with their contract, salary, induction, company training, etc. This will allow the managers and you to access this information easily.

Everything should be stored on open drives at all times to keep things organized. Using Google Drive or the cloud-based system means that you and your team can access all information needed at all times from any PC or anywhere in the world. Google Drive is great because, as the company owner, you are informed where your drive is being accessed from, at what time, and with which PC – that gives you complete control and flexibility over your systems. Since you are now controlling everything in your business without directly getting involved you can focus most of your time on the crucial tasks for driving your business forward. Finally, you've started working ON the business rather than IN the business.

In the next chapter, I will simplify one of the essential segments of your business – accounting! Having more cash flow in the business is essential. Therefore, you cannot skip this part even if you want to. Also, there is a free workbook waiting for you at the end of chapter 8. Don't miss out! It replenishes the lessons you learned in this book and helps you implement them. So, without further ado, let's get to it.

CHAPTER SEVEN

CASH IS KING! ACCOUNTING SIMPLIFIED

"The word accounting comes from the word accountability. If you are going to be rich, you need to be accountable for your money."

– Robert Kiyosaki

Finance is an essential element of your business. No business can survive, let alone scale, without cash flow. If you have a strong cash flow in hand, it's good news as you now have the flexibility to make effective business decisions regarding your investments. Your fundamental focus as the business owner should be channeled towards establishing healthy finances, or else nothing you do will matter; you will constantly feel stressed and worn out. Financial strain eliminates the pleasure you wish to attain from your business. Cash is the king! Furthermore, if your company has a healthy cash flow, mismanagement thereof could also affect the growth of your business. Therefore, this chapter is created to help you fix the financials of your business, acquire more cash flow, and manage it to gain explosive growth effortlessly.

A healthy financial business begins with a single bank account. It means you should have one business account for all your money to come in and go out. It will transform the end of a financial year into a hassle-free operation when submitting and paying taxes. I forbid you from using your personal bank account for your business; it doesn't matter how small the business is, open a separate account. Business is fun when you are paying yourself a salary; being the CEO of your business, you should pay yourself a fixed paycheck every month into your personal bank account. If you are to buy something for personal gain, use your personal account. Conversely, use your business bank account only if the transaction is for business purposes, such as a payment from your client or paying a supplier's invoice. Nevertheless, don't spend all your profits; whatever your business earns should be invested back into the business for growth and stability.

As your profits grow, you can pay yourself a higher salary. It is ubiquitous for business owners to be paid the lowest wage in comparison to the other employees in the beginning stages of the business. You need to hire exceptional talents that could lend you a hand in consistently growing and profiting the business. You are not the company, you are just an employee of your company, and you should treat yourself as such, learn to separate yourself and the business from the start. If you are unsure about your salary, ask yourself: "what can I pay to this employee for their service at the current level of my business? You will get your answer, and this is where separating you business from your personal entity helps. Look at the revenu coming in and subtract the expenses to get your profits. Whe paying your employees, you will estimate what amount of salary is suited for you.

You must do everything in your abilities to keep your expenses low. The manufacturing, shipping, or any cost you could cut, do it without cutting on quality. Have as much cash reserved as you possibly can. Get into the habit of questioning yourself before spending capital from your business account whether the purchase is necessary or not. Will it add value to the business? If NO, then don't do it. You can operate your company from anywhere in the world nowadays, so do you need a fancy office for everyone to work from? Instead, you could work remotely by implying a "work from home program." Live and run your business from a cheaper country and allow your staff the same flexibility. The excitement of working in this manner will sustain your team in your establishment for the long haul.

Find out if there is a cheaper country you could shift to save taxes, reduce expenditures. In addition, you should have at least three months of cash reserve to run your business for rainy days. Don't touch these funds unless unforeseen circumstances appear. Use the pandemic as an example. No one could foresee the world's situation when it hit, and all the businesses without emergency funds were wiped out – they are not opening their doors again.

On the other hand, you will see companies with a year of cash flow in reserve hopping back onto the market. You need to have these reserves for unpredicted circumstances. In my business, as an example, we had a client who ignored paying a substantial invoice for months. As a result, I required legal assistance. I had to fund all business expenses on top of the legal costs such as salaries, contractor's invoices, and other business costs, which was detrimental to my cash flow. I luckily had enough cash reserves to sustain the losses. In the end, the client declared bankruptcy, and my business never saw the payments. Have a strategy in place for such occasions so that you don't have to shut down or let your brilliant employees leave. It is just the ABCs of a healthy financial business. Warren Buffet said, *"accounting is the language of business"* – learn it.

GOOD DEBT V/S BAD DEBT

As soon as we hear the word debt, our head suddenly starts giving off mixed signals. Business owners like yourself need to understand that debt is not the devil here. You can use debt as leverage to take your business towards success. However, when debt is not appropriately managed, you could drown in a deep valley from which there is no coming back. That's why you must learn the difference between good and bad debt. Your company needs capital to grow its wings and fly to the seventh cloud - seeking financing or taking up a loan could give you the instant cash you need. The key here is to know when to go into debt an when to avoid it, which is where most businesses cripple; they take up the loan when they are at their lowest point. No revenue, no strategy, no recurring clients, and no innovation to disrupt the market.

Business owners feel that this is the point where debt is to be taken. That's a huge misconception; hoping that taking a loan will bring more clients and help them sustain themselves. Hope is not a business strategy – this is what I call terrible debt. Conversely, suppose you're on a roll and see an opportunity that would highly benefit the company, and you don't have the required capital to seize it. In that case, you can go ahead and apply for a loan because you know in the next 12 months, your business will be worth ten times more than it is now. It will be easy to pay back the loan. That is good debt. For example, you know that building a marketing team will add tremendous value to your company by establishing an online presence and running ads. So, you take on a loan, and your team will pay it off with their performance.

The government is encouraging startups to grow their businesses through multiple loan programs with lower interest rates. It's only because you're creating employment which in turn helps improve the economy. Taking a loan also keeps your company intact, which means that if you approach an investor for the same amount of money, they will take a big chunk of your business away. Taking a loan will enable you to have the required capital while remaining in full ownership of your company - it also helps reduce your taxes if the company is in debt. However, as we have already established, don't take on debt that your company can't pay back. I have been in that situation, done that, and got the t-shirt, and it's not a fun picture at all.

The amount of debt you require to reach your goals is not of concern if the outcome of that debt is a hefty return. The probability should always be in your favor, or else the debt is going to be a nightmare. Although, at this point, you know that you need someone to look after your business finances and advise you about the future steps. I suggest that you hire a Chief Finance Officer (CFO) or seek professional help. Provide them with your plan and take on their suggestions. However, if you can't afford a CFO at this stage, use your best judgment, go through the numbers and calculate the risk before applying for the loan.

Furthermore, if your business has already taken the debt and is now seeking a way out due to lack of control, here is a simple way to do so:

1. Lay down all the debts you have from the highest interest rates to the lowest. An organized view will tell you which debt to pay first (the one on the top).

2. Pump up your marketing strategy that will increase the sales in your business, which will automatically increase your profits and, in turn, assist you in paying off your debt. For example, you can run a limited-edition program.

3. Take on another loan and pay off the first one with a fixed interest rate – it's called refinancing the debt. Don't stay in high-interest rates debt for long because it will snowball into a crazy figure that will doom your business. Instead, start cutting costs, stop spending money without any returns, and do everything you can to get out of debt if you've already fallen into the trap.

4. Finally, analyze when you last increased your rates and jack up your prices. If your company is of value to your customers, your clients won't hesitate to buy premium when you raise your rates.

Most small business owners are afraid of increasing their prices because they fear losing their clients; I experienced the same trauma myself. It was scary to have those meetings, but my company added value; therefore, our clients didn't hesitate even though we increased our rates by 30% per booking. Now, I am not telling you to go this extreme, but work out what you think is fair based on the value your company offers and the problems it solves.

ACCOUNTING FOR BEGINNERS

As a business owner, there are a few accounting terms that you need to be aware of, and this section is designed to cover the basics. For example, do you know what a balance sheet is? It's an overview of all the assets, liabilities, and equity concerning your business. When your business is growing, it is a fun picture to look at and feel good. Conversely, you also have a profit and loss account, which will depict all the revenue coming in and the expenses going out. As a business owner, it is your responsibility to keep a tab on these accounts to know how much money your business will have at the end of the day.

When referring to profits, there are two types – gross profit and net income. Gross profit is the income that remains after subtracting production costs from revenue. The total income generated by selling products and services is called revenue which is how gross profits are calculated.

Gross profits = Revenue – Costs of goods sold

It is also referred to as gross income. Gross profit will let you know exactly how much profit your company is making at any given period. Gross refers to the amount of profits prior to any deductions. Conversely, net income is the profit that remains after subtracting all the business expenses and costs, including paying for software, salaries, etc.

Net Income = Revenue − All Costs and Expenses

Investors will be very interested in the Net income of your business. The Net Income will show how profitable your business is and how well it is being managed. After subtracting all expenses and taxes, Net income is the final figure, which is determined to calculate the earnings per share. Both the Gross profit and Net income can be used to establish whether your company is profitable or losing money. If the unfortunate is true, then where is the money going? While calculating your gross profits, keep in mind that the profits are also subject to taxes; therefore, your profits after tax deduction matter for the company's growth.

Another vital figure can be calculated from your gross profits, which is called gross profit margin. It signifies your production efficiency, meaning the number of products you could produce with the minimum time and resources. Even if your Gross profits are positive, if the cost of production or the time to create the number of products is doubled, your gross margins will fall big time, which is where most businesses lose focus. They are under the impression that their business is generating a good return until the end of the year when they are shocked by the actual figures. Gross profit margin is expressed in percentage and is calculated with the following formula:

Gross Profit margin = Revenue / Gross profits

You should focus on profits as it rewards all your hard work—the rainbow after heavy rainfall. There are multiple ways to escalate your profits, as mentioned earlier. Increase your sales per annum, attract new customers, cut costs that do not add direct value, remove products from your inventory that people have forgotten or are not interested in due to market trends, etc. These are just a few ways of how you could increase your business profits. Remember the 80/20% rule? It applies here too.

When your business is earning more money than spending, it is profitable, and its success will keep growing. Your business is considered successful if it has traction and growth. It means you're increasing your market capital and sales every year substantially, hiring employees, launching new products, etc. - the business's overall health is revealed through its profits and growth.

Another essential statement is the profit and loss statement that depicts all the profits gained and losses inflicted. You business performance is recorded into the financial statement, and it is one of the critical reports. Investors and stakeholders will decide your company's health based on the growth showcased in this report. Another crucial report is the cash flow statement which signifies where the money came from and went into your business. As the CEO, it is required to have all these reports available at arms-length to overview your business and its performance. In addition, you will be formulating your future strategies based on these reports.

CREATING BALANCE SHEET AND INCOME STATEMENT

A balance sheet is a swift view of equity, assets, and liabilities at a particular time in business. The balance sheet will have assets mentioned on the left side, and the right side will be liabilities and equity. Once you list it all down, you will have a concise image of your business. At the bottom of the sheet, you will have the total assets on the left and total liabilities and equity on the right. As the name suggests, both figures should be the same. The assets should match your liabilities plus equity figure – it is a problem if they both don't check. Luckily there are several software options available that allow us to gain an accurate balance that avoids error. Use effective software to save time and money. To always be on top of the finances in your business, I highly suggest you complete a balance sheet on a monthly, quarterly, and annually basis.

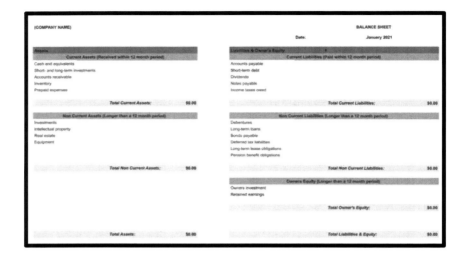

You can build a balance sheet yourself. As mentioned above, on the left is the list of assets, and on the right is the liabilities plus equity. An asset is an item that adds future economic value to your company, bringing money into the business. Conversely, liabilities are what your business owes, which takes the money out of your business. However, these categories are pretty broad, and you should know precisely what an asset is to your company and what is not. So let me give you a list of different types of assets.

There are two categories of assets, **current and non current assets.**:

1. The current assets are the assets that could be turned into cash quickly within 12 months—for instance, supplies, cash, inventory, etc.

2. Non-current assets take longer than 12 months to turn into cash or are difficult to convert—for instance, long-term investments, equipment, properties, etc.

The liabilities fall under the same category as assets: current and non-current liabilities:

1. The liabilities to be paid within 12 months are current liabilities, including salaries, taxes, accounts payable, accrued expenses, short-term loans, etc.

2. Liabilities that take longer than 12 months to settle are non-current liabilities, including long-term loans.

The final piece of the puzzle is equity. Owners' equity is the result of subtracting all the liabilities from the assets – the owners' rights upon the business shares. The second type of equity is called Retained earnings; it's the amount of net income left after subtracting all costs, liabilities, and paying dividends to all the shareholders and is reserved for future use.

MANAGING YOUR ACCOUNTANT AND BOOKKEEPER

A great accountant will help you comply with all the legal rules for taxes and accounting and provide a lending hand in the decision-making process of your finances. If you require their utmost support in the financial side of the business, they need to understand your objectives, goals, and vision and make it clear to them so that there are no issues in the future. Based on your business's finances, there are a few areas in which your accountant could assist you in deciding a product launch, research and development (R&D) expenditures, managing manufacturing costs, and any other area where money is involved. This additional level of support from your accountant usually comes at an extra cost.

Since accountants play such a crucial role in your business, it is common sense to take your time to find the best match for you and your company—one who will understand your business and believe in your vision. Then, run a survey among your colleagues, peers, and shortlist a few accounting firms. It is also advisable to use a social media platform such as LinkedIn to find great accountants because you can read testimonials and their profiles on these platforms.

Once you have shortlisted a few potential accountants, have a chat with them and ensure whether they are knowledgeabl about the industry in which you're running your business. It will be a bonus point for those who are, because they can provide you with some insights and will also be beneficial in highlighting upcoming opportunities. However, the most critical element is that they should be experts in their field and know all the essential core services accountants offer. Understand what is being provided as part of their package and try to negotiate for a long-term deal.

You will be in orderly contact with your accountant; if they have an off-putting personality that you dislike, perceive it as a red flag. Instead, find someone you get along well with, who explains everything clearly, who is open to discussion, and who could help you in every service you need. Do you feel at ease and comfortable around them? If yes, work with their establishment even if you have to pay a little extra for the best fit. It will save you much more money and hassle in the future – a great accountant will be involved in your business and call you with new ideas and questions; they won't wait for you to contact them for help.

If you're looking for online help without any human contact, there are multiple accounting software that will provide you with a one-stop accounting solution for you and your accountant. You can view all your business figures with a few taps on the screen. It comes in handy to be on the same page.

For example, if there is a decision to be made, you could both use the figures in the software as a baseline for discussion. Most accountants have their own software. If it fits well with your business operation, then hop on board. Keep your accountant clear on all the decisions you make, let them know what is important to you and what is not, and take their advice in the matter – a different perspective could be beneficial. Here are a few requirements to ensure that you're working with the best accountant there is:

- Set up a meeting after filing every tax and VAT return.
- Your accountant should explain all figures regarding your returns in full detail.
- Ensure that they are also pointing you towards all the obstacles that might come in your way, such as uncontrollable debt, account balance, etc.
- Make sure they provide you with advice on business growth, loans, or anything related to your company's finances.
- Ensure that they alert you about any necessary filing dates beforehand, maybe a few months in advance to avoid complications.
- Make sure your accountant prepares all your company reports and tax returns and submits them to you well in advance to re-verify all the numbers. I had faced terrible incident with my accountant in my recruitment

business. The company messed up my VAT return; I had calculated that I owed £5,000 VAT, but due to my accountant's mistake from earlier in the year, my VAT bill was £20,000 instead. However, as the CEO of my business, it was my mistake as well because I was too dependent on my accountant and didn't have much involvement at that stage. This lesson succored me to realize the vitality of knowing precisely what is happening on the financial side of my business. If I had been on top of my company finances as suggested in this chapter, I would have noticed the mistake and corrected it immediately; and I wouldn't have faced the massive bill months later. It hurt my business severely because I was only prepared for the payment of £5K.

- Once agreeing on the terms of your accountant's services, ensure they are agreed upon in writing. So, both parties sign the terms, making your agreement concrete evidence of their acceptance if you are faced with any issues later in the business relationship. Again, the terms should be discussed and agreed upon in the initial meeting.

DEVELOPING A FINANCIAL SYSTEM

Establishing effective systems and processes to monitor the financial health of your business and tax obligation is vital.

Follow this financial system to keep yourself organized and on top of managing financial-related tasks:

- **Step 1:** Create a finance folder in your company's cloud-based software like Google Drive or icloud, and label it "Financial."
- **Step 2:** Create subfolders inside the financial folder for each financial year, such as "2021".
- **Step 3:** Inside the yearly folders, create monthly folders for each financial year. For example, in the UK, the financial year runs from April to March.
- **Step 4:** Inside the monthly folders, create the following subfolders: bank statements, purchase invoices and sales invoices.
- **Step 5:** Save these monthly sales invoices, purchase invoices, and bank statements in each related monthly folder, respectively.
- **Step 6:** Create another subfolder in the financial folder and label it "Spreadsheets", save all the reports and spreadsheets (of exact spending and investing records etc.) in that folder.
- **Step 7:** If you're the investor in your business, the investments need to be recorded so that you can get you refund at a later date when your business is profitable Keep track of the investments via a spreadsheet, label i "Owners Investments." It is highly recommended t

invest capital into your business bank account and pay for business expenses via your business bank account only. Keep track of the investment amounts, dates invested, and via which bank account the investment was made (for example, if there are two business owners making investments from their personal accounts). Save the spreadsheet in the spreadsheet folder.

- **Step 8:** Use an Income statement and balance sheet to track all expenses and goods sold. Save the balance sheet in your spreadsheet folder.

- **Step 9:** Schedule a day weekly or an hour daily in your default diary to manage your finances better, update your spreadsheets, issue invoices, and keep track of all expenses. Make financial management a habit so that your business's finances are always organized. You don't want to waste time accumulating all this information for your accountant to perform your tax returns at the end of the financial year.

- **Step 10:** Share the entire financial folder with your accountant and bookkeeper so that they always have access to your company's financials, and no delays are slowing them down from their job at any stage. It will also prevent any unknown issues from occurring.

- **Step 11:** Always know your numbers and the amount payable for tax and VAT returns. Be a wise business person to avoid any nasty surprises.

- **Step 12:** It is advisable to create another folder in the financial folder labeled "Legalities" and save company information from the tax office in this folder, including your tax number, company registration, etc. There is nothing more aggravating than approaching the end of the financial year, needing to submit your tax returns, and not finding the letterhead with your company tax registration number etc.

- **Step 13:** Create a spreadsheet of all your business passwords, login information, and company access codes related to submitting your tax returns and company registration so that you and your accountant has access to this information at all times and is easily accessible. Save it in the "legalities" folder with all the relevant documentation. You will be surprised how much time this process will save you and how many times you will need to access this information. You will thank me one day.

BENEFITS OF USING ACCOUNTING SOFTWARE

Accounting software is one of the most recommended tools in your financial arsenal. It will help you keep track of your invoices, clients, bank accounts and provide you with a insightful report. The first benefit of accounting software is the ease of storing all invoices and billings. We all know how tedious and time-consuming it is to maintain our billings and invoice on physical paper. If you misplace some of this information, it could wreck up your entire financial year. The software enables you to create recurring invoicing from one particular client with just a few taps. It's far more accessible and practical. You can even schedule the invoices for your customers. It will remind your customers regarding their payments, track all their invoices, and automate your payment-related tasks, saving you time and money.

The second benefit is the ease of collecting payments from customers by integrating your accounting software with payment gateways to give your customers an option to pay online, which will hold the records of revenues from the clients and customers. For a global business, get ready to accept all payment methods, whether credit card, debit card, direct bank transfer from multiple currencies, or even cryptocurrencies. Staying up to date will entice your customers to stay with your company for the long haul.

The third benefit of using software is the ability to track all the expenses from one place. In addition, the software will fill your cash flow statement, eliminating paper storing. The fourth benefit is that you can connect your bank account to the software, and it provides a streamlined approach to fetch and verify the statements – hence, it keeps your business audit-ready at any time of the year.

The fifth benefit is a timesheet module that helps you keep track of your time with each client. If you are consulting hourly, it is now easier to keep track of your time to avoid underbilling or overbilling your client. After completing the project, you can have an overview report of the total hours worked and the utilized budget to plan the next project appropriately.

The sixth benefit is inventory management. It is essential to have sufficient stock of the items per customer demands to keep your customers happy. It will record the item information, track the stock, provide reports, and notify you when to restock your inventory. You can also construct an automatic email to your manufacturer to always have sufficient supply to fulfill orders.

Helping you to be more tax compliant is the 7th benefit of using accounting software. It will work in conjunction with your tax laws and help you manage your returns accurately. It will give you a concise view of the returns, generate summary reports, and save a lot of your time. Looking at your generated reports will help you to have the insights and stay in the safe zone.

The three most important statements for your business are the cash flow statement, balance sheet, and profit and loss statement, it can all be generated using accounting software. Apart from these statements, you will also have a detailed view of your sales, inventory, taxes, projects, etc. As a result, you will make better-informed decisions and keep your business healthy. I understand that it may sometimes be overwhelming, dealing with numbers, revising reports, etc. however, your business depends on you making better financial decisions.

You cannot do that unless you have all your facts straight, and that's why you need to put your head down and hammer it all in and hire an accountant to assist you. Either way, you must have this section under control for a successfully growing business.

"Don't ever let your business get ahead of the financial side of your business: accounting, accounting, accounting. Know your numbers." – Tilman J. Fertitta.

We are finally down to the last chapter of this fantastic book, which is dedicated to helping you guide your marketing team towards success. The way you market your business is everything. Don't forget about the powerful workbook that I promised you for free at the end of the last chapter. Need raving fans? Let's proceed together!

CHAPTER EIGHT

FROM RAVING FANS TO MARKETING

"Marketing strategy is where we play and how we win in the market. Tactics are how we can deliver on the strategy and execute for success."

— Mark Ritson

Strategic marketing often results in business growth. If you can successfully educate your customers, engage them well, and create a solid reputation of your company in their minds, your business will most likely do well. On top of that, businesses thrive on acquiring new customers. If you want to promote your business, you need to use the three mystic tools: branding, advertising, and marketing. This chapter will help you guide your marketing team in the right direction to attract customers and turn them into raving fans — in turn, driving sales and explosive profits.

Are you at a point in your business that your cash flow isn't consistent? In some months, you have an influx of new leads and clients, while in some months, not so much? Well, this is probably because your business is at a stage where you are only relying on word of mouth, and on top of that, you think that this is enough to grow your business; apparently, it is not. You must overcome this mindset to scale up successfully. Nevertheless, the inconsistent leads and cash flow are an example that you need something more. This chapter will go over the importance of having a solid marketing strategy in place where word of mouth is only one of your funnels.

Your main objective should be to retain customers, so they keep buying from you to magnify your revenue. Unfortunately, most business owners confuse the three mystic tools and use them interchangeably. However, no sealing could stop you from going through the roof when you unlock the real difference between them and use them at the highest level. Therefore, let me help you understand the difference between each of the tools to utilize them effectively. Branding is not just some colors and a cool logo; it is what you believe in and stand for in the marketplace. It is about making a statement that you exist, how people perceive you, and what they feel about your company and products. Do you want people to stay loyal to your company? Let them know the purpose of your business through branding.

How do you stand out from the crowd? First, get you purpose straight and convey it through visual components Regardless of how opposed you are to it; people do judge a boo by its cover. Hence, having a polished look makes a crispy firs impression. The visual components of branding include a logc color codes, name, tagline, etc. Make it so appealing that peopl remember you the minute they look at your company. The McDonald's brothers discovered that red and yellow make people happy and stand out; for them, these colors signify food, they've been using these colors ever since. Branding is the battle of aligning your customer's perspectives with your business or instead finding a group of people who already have the same perspective – I'll let that sink in; it's deep.

Conversely, marketing is how you create awareness about your business, the strategies you come up with, how you sell your products, how you portray your brand, all of which come under marketing. Whether positive or negative, every word about the company is a form of marketing; if someone talks about your organization, they give you a marketing boost. As a business owner, it is your job to train your team to provide excellent customer service so that the message conveyed about your company is positive; leverage the message as a word-of-mouth campaign. Marketing also includes the social media presence, customer service, relationship building, website, and every document that has your company's logo printed on it.

Finally, advertising is only a subset of marketing that helps you magnify your sales and acquire new customers. Any content curated with your target audience in mind and then paid to be showcased on multiple channels to grab their attention is advertising. Advertising includes all outlets such as social media, newspaper, magazine, TV, radio, posters, etc.

BUILDING A BRAND BIBLE

When creating a solid brand, specific guidelines are required to maintain your identity, the voice of your business, and your business's personality. The brand bible is a book that provides unique guidelines for your business's marketing, advertising, and internal and external communication. It includes color schemes, designs, and fonts. In addition, the book will be used to design everything in your business from the website, logo, emails, welcome packs for clients, systems, and processes for your team; you get the picture.

To build an identity, create awareness, and let people know that all the content they are seeing is coming from the same business, you need to be consistent in the branding and stick to it like a permanent adhesive. Every business has a brand bible from top billion-dollar brands to new startups. The length of this document depends on your company. However, you can refer to it as a "set of rules" designed to keep your message uniform across all platforms.

Having a brand bible makes it easier to communicate the message you convey to your customers and what people are saying about your brand. In addition, all the marketing elements could be handled using this one document – your designers and marketing team will use it when creating new marketing material. It is advised that your marketing team design the book before developing your company branding to follow the guidelines.

Fonts

The brand bible describes which fonts are used within your brand and how to use them – play around with the fonts and styles and choose the best fonts that define your brand and stick with them forever – You can use different fonts, for example, for your logo and emails. However, don't go overboard; you don't want to have more than five fonts throughout all your branding.

Colors

One of the highlighting factors of your brand is the color code you use to display your beliefs and understanding of the market needs. Select a few colors as you did with fonts and use them every time. For example, Starbucks uses a deep green color on a white background to signify the positive nature of the brand and how it treats its customers every time they walk in; their partners and stakeholders. Ensure that your brand bible has minimum color palettes with names, color value, RGB value, and HEX value.

Images

The brand bible also specifies the type of images you will use to define your brand, whether actual photography, graphics, or illustrations. Then, there will be clear-cut instructions on how to edit them and use them. For example, Nike uses high-contrast images to stand out and draw customers in – be consistent and unique.

Furthermore, list down all the words you want your brand to be associated with. Words such as integrity, quality, assurance, efficiency, etc., project it into the consumer's minds, so your brand words are used when describing your brand. I believe that branding is a splendid way to inform people what to say about your organization. It holds power, and it has significance. You can look at Nike, Skype, Intel, I Love NY, etc., for inspiration. The following elements should be present in your brand bible: the purpose and vision of the brand along with the history, logo and its usage, fonts, colors schemes, image specifications, brochure rules, business card designs, voice and writing style, social media rules, and examples of each for your employees to understand.

Explore your horizons, set rules, and encourage your team to be creative; stick to the guideline but don't be too strict to limit your options and creativity. Always remember, the ultimate goal of your brand is to tell your story and stick in the minds of your customers.

THE UNIQUE SELLING PROPOSITION (USP)

Your business must have a unique feature or capability that none of your competitors possess. Why should consumers invest their money in buying your products if there are multiple products out there similar to yours? You must have a cutting-edge in:

- The way you manufacture your products; the purpose you're trying to perceive; the ingredients you use;
- The price point you offer your products or services at;
- Or any other feature that will convince your target audience to buy your products.

The sooner you can communicate your USP with your customers, the better. It defines your position in the market, the problem you solve, and how you do it. Sometimes, people don't know what they want; take the plunge and tell them why your product is better than what the market offers. Make it very clear from day one, and you will have an organization booming in affluence.

For instance, there is nothing new about selling shoes online, but the free return policy makes Zappos stand out from the crowd. You won't be charged to return the pair of shoes you don't like – that's their USP. Nike also sells shoes like other brands, but their USP is quality and focuses on celebrity endorsement. They specially design their shoes for athletes and consumers who are indulged in fitness. Your most significant achievement will be associating your brand name with your USP. People should recognize your business based on the USP. To achieve that, you need to communicate your USP effectively through social media, advertising, content marketing, search engine optimization (SEO), and digital marketing – spreading the word like fire.

It is not always easy to know exactly what drives people to buy your products. In today's world, everything is quantifiable. One of the ways you could find out your USP is through A/b testing. It's a trial-and-error method of testing your products. You can create multiple landing pages on your website and showcase your product with different attributes. The page with the highest traffic and, most importantly, conversion (sales) wil tell you which feature to highlight in the next campaign and ever after.

Steps To Create A USP For Your Business

After being enticed with the concept of USP, you must b waiting for me to give you specific hand-holding in creating USP for your business, aren't you? I can't let you down now, ca I? Here is a step-by-step process for creating a USP for you business.

- **Step 1:** Know your target audience. It is imperative because understanding your target audience is where selling begins. We will discuss about creating audience personas in later sections, but for now, you must know who your target audience is, their age, location, interest, and gender.

- **Step 2:** List the features, benefits, and attributes your product provides. Know what your product can do and how your product solves your customers' problems. Now, cross off all the benefits that are already offered by your competitors. Your USP must represent something your company is exceptionally better or faster at, making your business stand from your competitors.

- **Step 3:** Conduct a research study with a group of people familiar with your company to test if they agree with the USP you have created. Provide them with the USP to analyze their reaction; if their response is positive, use that USP in your company.

- **Step 4:** Verify whether your selected USP matches your business. Is it easily memorable? Is it direct and clear? Can you deliver the promise you're claiming in that USP? The answer should be YES to all of these questions.

- **Step 5:** Position and market your brand based on your business's Unique Selling Proposition (USP). Add it into your marketing strategy, use it as a benchmark to be at the forefront of your customer's mind.

When it works, and people are turning into customers, it's no time to rest; keep monitoring and stay on top of all the latest trends because getting to the top is one thing but staying on top is a different game.

VALUE PROPOSITION IN YOUR BUSINESS

In the most basic form, it is the value your customers gain from your product or service. It is essentially the promise your brand makes and is backed up with results. The value proposition is the reason your customers purchase your products over your rival's products. The more compelling and engaging your value proposition is, the more people will line up to buy from you – make sure to state all the benefits of your product. For instance, if you're selling a delicious donut and people love it, they might buy a few, but this alone isn't enough to be unique. However, if your branding is that you sell a healthier version of a regular donut this is when you start to stand out from the crowd. The health benefits conserved with a pinch of deliciousness are you value proposition and also a USP. To take your value a step further, you might be among the few donut makers who accept online orders and free home delivery. You can communicate your value proposition through words, images, videos, etc. Use your Value Proposition to stand out from the crowd.

There is no solid format for creating a value proposition. However, there is a structural model that might come in handy. Let me share it with you. It begins with an attention-grabbing headline. Keep it concise, simple, and use numbers to build credibility. Next, it must outline your single most crucial proposition. Follow it up with bulleted benefits and features to explain your core feature. You can then add short, engaging content to draw your target audience in, give a concise version of your product, and tell the market how it's better than what's already out there. Always remember, don't promise something you can't deliver. Saying that you are the cheapest is not a value because anyone with deeper pockets than yours could launch the same product at more affordable rates. You will lose your edge and customers. It is best to underpromise and overdeliver, then the other way around.

Finally, end with social proof and customer reviews to build trust. Video testimonials on your website and written Google reviews are the best ways to receive reviews. However, written reviews on your website don't hold much value if your brand is not yet well known. Be creative in the way you ask your customers to leave a feedback on your business. For example, in my recruitment business, we ran a promotion. For every honest review we received by the end of the promotion, we donated £10 to a charity of their choice. In today's social media world, if your company doesn't have reviews, it holds no value in the market.

So, gaining feedback should be on the top of your goal list. In the long run, it is the best way to gain new customers.

CREATING A MARKETING STRATEGY FOR YOUR TEAM

Everything you do to create awareness, attract customers, and retain them is called marketing. Your customers have no idea that you exist. The only way to let them know about your company is through marketing – spread the word that there is a company with strong culture and values, ready to capitalize. People sometimes confuse marketing with advertising and public relations. They are just a subset of the entire picture. For a person to become your customer, there are a few steps they have to take to qualify. This path is referred to as the marketing funnel. One of the most well-known funnels is named the AIDA model, introduced by Elias St. Elmo Lewis.

In the basic form, AIDA refers to Awareness, Interest Desire, and Action. You can modify it according to your need for sales, conversion, or purchase funnel. Simply put, at the outermost layer is the awareness, where you spread the word about your business, and those who're interested will follow through into the funnel. Then they transition into the third phase, which is desire. If people are interested but have no desire to buy or see no real value, they will move out.

Conversely, when they have the desire to buy and use the product, if it solves a significant problem they've been suffering with, then they will take action. It is your job to train your employees to transition your target audience into actual customers. Regardless of the model you follow, remember that a funnel has one primary motive, to convert non-customers into customers and encourage them to take action (make a purchase) – there will be some people who will jump off the funnel, and that is expected, however, make the process as smooth and easy as possible so that they are naturally drawn into it.

It is crucial to monitor the funnel process and discern the area where the majority of the people drop off. Of course, you can't please everyone, but if you can improve, do it. For instance, your marketing spreads awareness; it caught the audience's interest, and they clicked on your website; however, they clicked away the moment they landed on your page, which means your website or landing page didn't fulfill their interest and failed to spark their desires; therefore, they lost attention. Consequently, you need to improve where your funnel is losing the interest of your audience so that more people will follow through and take action (make a purchase).

Marketing Funnel

There is good news and bad news for you. Which one would you like to hear first? The good news is that there are multiple ways to create awareness and peak interest in your product in the marketplace. The bad news is that most people screw it up because of their lack of focus and inability to leverage the full potential of these methods. I want you to be among the few companies who gain access to this market and make the best use of these funnels. Here are the golden approaches that hold the key to your marketing success:

- **Content marketing**: It involves curating engaging and innovative content in multiple forms such as blogs, social media posts, videos, etc. Everything that you write online or traditionally about your product and services or business is content marketing. For example, the caption on the Instagram post, a video on Facebook, ads on LinkedIn, or the content on your website all of these funnels fall under content marketing.

- **Social media marketing**: This approach uses social media sites to create awareness and enhance brand recognition. Notable platforms like YouTube, Facebook, Instagram, Linked In, Pinterest, Twitter, Tumblr, and every other social media channel are used to conduct a marketing preview. It works so effectively because the make it super easy to share posts with friends and families. A smart business owner knows that they need to establish a social media presence to boost marketing

- **Email marketing**: It is the process of collecting emails by providing value. When you have many emails, you know this audience is interested in your product and services. You can then send out weekly newsletters to communicate with them directly. Warren Buffet said that money is in the list. Those who leverage email marketing always make their way into the league of success.

- **Public relations**: PR is a sophisticated method to build a solid relationship and reputation of your business with influencers, journalists, and more. PR is where you tell your story and get them hooked to your brand. PR isn't by any means cheap, but it should pay for itself, as should all your marketing methods and team.

- **Search engine optimization**: SEO is an organic way to build credibility. When a potential customer searches for a term on Google or other search engines, and your product or website shows up, you will gain heavy traffic and advertisement without spending a dime on ads. Link building is not an easy job and takes time to see results, but having a solid team to back you up could take you to the first page of Google. The first step is to choose a unique name that isn't already available online (this should be your company name). Then, you conduct thorough research to find all the key terms people type in the search engine using various software like Google keyword planner, Semrush, etc. You have both free and paid versions available. However, your marketing team or SEO manager should conduct the keyword searches and suggest the best software for your company within the budget.

- **Advertising**: This is a paid method of letting people know about your products. Running paid promotions on social media, search engines, or print ads enables you to reach a broader audience in the minimum time possible.

- **Integrity**: No matter which approach you use, without integrity, everything else is irrelevant. Speak the truth, and don't backstab your customers by selling a not-so-great or low-quality product or by overpromising. Don't use unethical ways to get clients and customers; they will abandon you for good once they find out. A great business is built on trust and integrity.

Your task now is to sit and sketch a marketing funnel for your business; then, you can choose any marketing approach you like or a combination of a few. Whatever suits you business, do it. It is also essential to track all your marketing efforts and analyze which generates more leads. Why? So that you can eliminate the ones that don't work to save your time and money. Remember, be focused on finding the 20% that make up for 80% of your outcomes (Pareto principle).

7 Steps Marketing Strategy

It is not always 100% guaranteed that your marketing strategy will work. It is a lot of trial and error. So, how can you be sure that the marketing strategy you create bears fruit? It is because I decided to give you a step-by-step guide to create an effective strategy. My job is to show you the right path and walk beside you; I can't walk for you. Hence, use these steps to begin creating history:

Step 1: Create a marketing plan

A strategy without a plan is a recipe for failure. You may be wondering if you need a plan for your strategy? And the answer is YES. Your strategy is the overview of the process that your team will be needing to perform. The actions they will take, the resources they will use, and the goals they will achieve. Conversely, a marketing plan is your team's exact actions to enforce a successful strategy. A plan includes your budget for marketing, the action steps to take, the approaches to utilize, and the tasks to implement to gain the upper hand and achieve your goals.

Step 2: Create a customer's image

This step involves creating a persona for your ideal customers. Before you launch a product, you must know who it is for, the demographics, gender, country, age, etc. you can't sell roller skates with a persona of a 60 years old man. Know who the customer really is and create a persona. For example, suppose you're selling designer clothes at a 50% discount. In that case, your customer persona is Gracia, a 24 years old woman from the UK who works in a corporate job and wants to fill her closet with beautiful designer dresses at affordable prices. You should give names to your persona and describe the age, interest, job title, and problem faced, etc. I did my research, and here you are, reading my book after all, from cover to cover - persona success!

Step 3: Understand your goals

We already created goals for your business in chapter 3. Use them here. Your marketing strategy needs to be focused on achieving your business goals. For example, if your goal is to gain 10,000 customers in 10 months, you can channel your marketing efforts and use the above approaches to build awareness and a pool of 1000 potential customers every month Whatever your goals are, think about whether your marketing is helping you to achieve them or not.

Step 4: Use effective tools

Your determination is plausible, but not having the right tool to match your vision could be catastrophic. Find the right tool for your business to improve your processes, make them efficient, and help you achieve your goals quicker. Use scheduling tools for your social media posts, gain analytics, and keep track of your audience. Measure your traffic on you website and blog with google analytics or other software and online platforms like Trello, Buzzsumo, Hubspot, or Crazy Egg to stay in touch with your team and keep a tab on your processes. While some are free, some are paid, and some require in-app purchases to avail more features. Your marketing team must guide you appropriately to use proper software while keeping the company's budget in mind.

Step 5: Scrutinize existing resources

Examine all the resources you already have available within your grasp that you could leverage to gain traction. What can you use to curate a formidable strategy? For example, look out for the awareness you built around social media and other platforms using paid ads or the audience you built using your email list, blogs, ebooks, etc., or the buzz you earned for your business through social shares and tweets from other people online. Gather all the resources in one place and segregate them to decide what can be used.

Step 6: Inspect and plan

After you gather all the available resources, discard the ones that aren't useful to you in any way and focus all your efforts on the ones that are. Keep a keen focus on the audience you built and the goals you have. Next, verify your customer's image you created before. If there is a challenge your person is facing, try to find solutions to help them out. Finally, plan all content upfront with a title, content, purpose, and expectations.

Step 7: Take massive action and achieve your goals

You now have a clear idea of how your plan will bear fruit. Bring all your research and steps together and put them into action. Define your strategy and monitor your movements. If something could be polished, do it in the initial stages. This simple act should benefit you for a long-long time. Use these seven steps and create an amazing marketing strategy that will bring you results without wasting too much of your time, money, and resources.

LEAD GENERATION

Lead generation is the process of finding potential customers and attracting them to your marketing funnel. Every person that comes into your funnel is a potential prospect that holds the ability to be converted into a loyal customer. That's the reason why lead generation is one of the vital components of marketing strategy. If you don't have a marketing team yet, you can outsource it to a marketing agency. Understanding your target audience, interest, where they hang out, what they read, and other information is key to your business growth. You must always know how many people come knocking on your door (leads) and how many enter your house (conversion rate).

One of the best platforms to get leads is social media. There are billions of people on it every day; all you have to do is come up in front of them, entice them with your offer, and tell them how to make a simple purchase. It works for both B2B and B2C markets. The only difference will be the platforms you use. If you are selling directly to customers, you can use Facebook, Instagram, Pinterest, etc. However, if you are selling your products to businesses (B2B), you can use LinkedIn, Twitter, etc.

If someone is interested in your product or services, it's called a lead. For example, you can offer a free ebook on a crash course you just made and collect their email addresses in return. If they download your ebook, you know they are interested, and now you can send them a weekly newsletter giving more valuable information about your business. It is relatively easy on social media because people have already filled out their bios on each platform. When they approach your product, you can look at their profile and qualify to pull them further into the funnel. The more leads you get, the higher the conversion rate. Using social media will amplify your lead generation process.

How To Generate Leads from Social-Media?

There are 3.96 billion people active on social media. Since it plays a crucial role in magnifying your impact, let's see how it can be used to build valuable leads. As mentioned before, you need to have a unique hook offer, mostly free giveaways that people could download for free. It can be a case study, ebook, a free webinar, discount codes, or anything valuable. It must be free, but it should be helpful to them. When your company offers this much value for free, the target audience will wonder what you could provide in exchange for money. They must be curious and enticed by your lead magnet. You can further build more credibility by showcasing social proof from people who've seen tremendous results from your product or service.

The next thing you should do is create ads. Your team needs to be marketing your products across all platforms like Facebook, Instagram, Google, YouTube, LinkedIn, Twitter, etc. Depending on your target audience, your team should be creating an appealing ad to bring in more customers. Every platform has its way of setting up the ads system, your content changes with the type of ad you wish to display as well. For example, with YouTube and Facebook, it's more of a video sponsored ad that works. However, Instagram focuses on pictures instead. Find out where your customers hang out and target them effectively. If you don't have a dedicated marketing team yet, you should focus on setting up a team, or you will have to create the ad by yourself until you have a dedicated team. Canva.com is a great place to create content for ads.

Ads always have a wider reach than organic posts. If you add your special one-time offer and advertise it, you will see a pool of leads leaning towards you. For example, a food delivery company ran an Instagram ad giving 70% off on the first three orders. People ordered like crazy, giving them a massive opportunity to showcase how efficient their delivery services were. After the third purchase, people were already hooked to the service. How could you create the same effect with your business? Think again! If you are not getting any leads, it means something isn't working. You need to use the trial-and-error method to figure out what it is, tweak it a little bit, or change it entirely until you start generating leads. That's how you get a successful system in place.

Another concept within the social media marketing is retargeting. Your ad will be shown to millions of people, but not all who are interested will take immediate action. Therefore, ad software provides you the chance to catch those missed leads by retargeting them. For example, maybe someone spent too much time on your post and read it but didn't take any action, or someone clicked your ad and landed upon your website but then left, or maybe someone reads your blogs every week but never subscribes. You can retarget all these people again. Since they already displayed interest, the chances are that they are more likely to purchase the next time they click on your ad.

This small technique could increase your conversion rate by ten times (10x) or more – use the AIDA marketing funnel to capture leads and convert them into customers. When your marketing team performs well and bring in leads, the lead can then be passed to your sales team, where they will provide them with more valuable content, nurture them, make them aware of your brand and products, and convert them into a client. The more deals your sales team converts, the more profitable your company will be. It is vital that your marketing and sales team work in harmony for this technique to be successful. One team is responsible for bringing in the leads, and the other is responsible for converting the lead and ensuring they remain a client. Therefore, train your employees with appropriate systems and processes to help them close as many deals as possible and convert many leads into customers.

As the business owner, you should know exactly how many leads are coming in and being converted; and why the leads that weren't successful didn't convert so that you can improve in those areas. The non-conversion rates should be discussed in weekly team meetings with your sales and marketing team. Knowledge is power, especially in this element of your business - know your numbers!

DELIVERY MASTER

Delivery mastery is all about getting your product in the hands of your customers while maintaining the promise you made to them. A crucial element is delivering the promise you made to your customer on or before the set timeline. For example, how do you feel when you order a product online, and the company emails you on the expected delivery date to inform you that they are running late with your delivery? It causes frustration, right? Especially when you've been excited to get your hands on that product or if it was a gift for someone special on their birthday. It leaves a sour taste in your mouth, and chances are, you wouldn't use their services again, and even worse, you will spread the word about your bad experience to your peers and family members; jeopardizing that company's reputation. This is what delivery mastery is all about—keeping the promise your company makes so that your customers are happy and spread the word about your business. Therefore, creating raving fans!

Always remember, when a customer is happy, they will speak about your business to 10 friends. However, when they are unhappy, they will talk about your business to 1000 people. Therefore, don't make promises your business can't fulfill. In relation, there are four main areas you need to thrive in if you want people to talk positively regarding your services:

- **Supply**: Ensure that your inventory is stocked timely. For example, if you suddenly get an order for 10,000 products, you should be able to fulfill them. Your deliveries must be consistent. You should never have to inform your clients that you can't meet their orders. Once they leave, don't expect them to return if you could not complete their order, especially if they are a first-time client.

- **Quality**: Whenever a customer receives an inferior product, it frustrates them. They will not only retract their order and demand their money back; they will spread the word about you on social media and any other means necessary. Therefore, your product or service should always be top quality. For example, McDonald's consistently makes the same quality food irrelevant to the country because of the systems they have in place. Therefore, ensure that your business provides consistent quality.

- **Ease of purchase**: Whether we want to admit it or not, we are getting lazier by the day. Therefore, the process to complete an order purchase should be straightforward. The minute you add another step or make the process complicated, you will lose the customer for good. The easier it is to buy from your company, the greater the potential you hold to scale. Review your purchase page; if it currently takes five steps to fulfill an order, are you able to narrow it down to two or one step? The faster a potential customer can buy from your company, the more revenue you will generate. Having a quick payment structure is also extremely beneficial for consumers to make an impulse purchase. If your payment process takes too long, the consumer's interest span evaporates, and they might go to your competitor. It is well known that Facebook advertisements can be very impulsive and triggered purchases.

- **Service**: Customer service is everything. Your team's work doesn't end when you get your customers money and fulfill their orders. The relationship only begins at this point. How your customer service is handled in your business will be revealed through your customer retention rate. Are you creating a wow-effect? Do your customers smile after getting off a call with one of your executives? Do they love your service? Of course, they must; because if they don't, you need some significant improvements in this area of your business. Deliver the service you promised, stand firm, and people will notice.

Make your customers feel valued and appreciated. Just because you have 100,000 customers doesn't give you a right to neglect 5 loyal customers. For example, in my recruitment business, as a thank you to our clients every Christmas we gave the decision-making clients in each team a spa gift voucher in a five-star spa of their choice, which not only made us stand out from our competitors but also made us at the forefront of our client's mind when making decisions about which company to use.

Your business needs a foundation upon which it thrives. These foundations are divided into four strong pillars: the owners, staff, suppliers, and clients/customers. Each of them thirsts for nurturing and needs specific elements to function effectively. The owners want to see business scale and make explosive profits. Your staff needs recognition, feel valuable, and need a steadily growing paycheck. Your suppliers want their bills to be paid on time. Finally, your customers want to fulfill their needs and problems to be solved, and your clients provide nourishment to all the other three pillars.

Training Your Staff Is Vital

As mentioned before, your customers must feel great after getting off the phone with your staff members. You need to train them well to speak politely to your customers, tend to their needs, and help them solve every query they have because every interaction with your customer is a massive opportunity for growth. Understand your goals and what works for your business because every business is unique. Use the previous stated areas of the business to guide you to your successful customer experience. Set the standards high for your business and meet them every single time. Hold your team accountable for every customer interaction they handle, and you will see your company mastering the art of delivery. Bravo!

CREATING RAVING FANS

You are already aware of the Pareto principle we discussed in the initial chapters, aren't you? 80% of your profits come from 20% of your customers. Building a raving fan base is all about the Pareto principle. Chances are, only 20% of your customers are generating 80% of your revenue. Imagine how efficiently your business would run if you had 1000 raving fans? Hold on to that adrenaline because now I will teach you how to create a "Raving Fans" process that your team can easily follow. This process involves mastering delivery, as customer experience is everything.

- **Step 1**: List all the platforms and areas of interface your team has with your target customers, including social media, advertising, email, etc. Set expectations for each point of contact. Learn what your customers want, how they feel, and what they expect from your business. What will make their journey go from "just great" to "incredibly amazing"? Conduct a survey regarding the quality of your services to gain direct feedback from your customers and use the feedback to improve your customer experience.

- **Step 2**: Fulfill your customers' demands so that you stand out from your competitor. It is OK if you can't meet every minutely detailed expectation of your customer; there could be many reasons for that, which I can appreciate, but make sure that you exceed their primary expectations to such a degree that they willingly give you their credit card with a smile on their face.

- **Step 3**: Once you have developed a new process from the suggestions above, this is the step where you outline exactly what will be included in the process and how it will be implemented. Know who will be doing the implementation and the outcome that will be gained after execution. Communicate your and your customer's needs clearly to your team and let them make it happen.

- **Step 4**: This step implies goals associated with every customer experience. Be very specific in providing the projected goals to your employees regarding you customer's expectations. For example, setting a goal to deliver a product with a 95% compliance rate mean fulfilling 95% of your customer's deliveries as promised That's a great figure to achieve.

- **Step 5**: Hold your team accountable to fulfill these goal and provide them with the tools needed to achieve th goals efficiently.

- **Step 6**: Communicate with your team how you wi measure their performance. Having a process ready is a outstanding achievement. Now is the time to set a specific timeline within which the process will be executed. Outline when the testing will be held, when the review will take place, and when you will officially roll out the process. Include everything that will be required for a smoother process.

- **Step 7**: Set a concrete measure for your customer's reaction to the newly enhanced process. You can post surveys, add a referral program, and conduct research for feedback on the process.

- **Step 8**: The final step towards creating raving fans is to note that the effective process you curated can be sustained until it is replaced with a newer, improved version. Each outlet and department in your business should integrate this enhanced process to provide a consistent qualitative experience to your customers.

I believe that if new processes aren't measured, tested, and installed, they will perish into thin air. Change is not always accepted right away, some employees might resist your enhancement, and some might take longer to adapt. In any case, communicating the new processes and backing it up with reasons will give you an upper hand if this situation arises. It's OK if your entire team isn't on board with the new process initially, persist and make it happen anyways. If you win, you will have the last laugh, and if you don't, you will learn a lesson for a lifetime. There is no failure in the business world, only lessons.

Following these eight steps thoroughly will help your business obtain raving fans. Keep your guard up with the customer experience model and keep improvising. Stillness isn't accepted in business. You either walk forward or run backward – what do you choose?

SALES

It is believed that customers are superior to business owners because they pay for the product or the service. However, I think that it is an equal two-way relationship. They aren't doing any favors for your business because your business should be solving a problem for them in exchange for a small fee. Knowing that, let's explore the sales sector to understand what it is, why it's essential, the key strategies, and what you can do to enhance the sales in your business. You cannot help your clients unless they buy from you. That's why sales play a vital role in building trust and loyalty between the two parties. When your business presents excellent customer service, it encourages your customer to spread the word about your services and refer friend who will spread the word too. Your revenues will skyrocket when you commit to the successful selling of your products.

The sole purpose of your sales team is to convert a lead that generates revenue for your business; otherwise, why are they part of your team? Remember the leads we attracted using the marketing funnel? Sales are the next stage of that funnel. The last "action" phase is when the funnel's lead is converted into a client. All that is required is a little more information and a gentle push toward the purchase. For example, let's say you want to buy a suit for a big presentation. You walked into a clothing store that a friend recommended and browsed your options. When entering the store, you know you want a tailored fitted suit that you need to receive back within two weeks. You've heard the name and quality claims of the shop. You are confident that you will find the best suit in that shop. However, you are not sure which suit to choose, there are so many great options. A salesperson approaches you with a smile and greets you respectfully. She asks, "what are you looking for? May I assist you?" You reply, "I just want to get a nice suit for a big presentation."

The saleswoman then guides you through the range of options based on your requirements, shows you images of models in the suits you like the most, and then informs you that you can have a tailored suit in your favorite color in the next week. Maybe she even upsells you a pair of shoes that fits well and feels comfortable. She even offers a 15% discount to match your budget. What will you say? Hell yeah! You are more likely to follow through with the transaction and feel good about it when you receive a high-quality product and excellent customer service. More importantly, you will be a raving fan and loyal customer for the years to come. You might even give the store a positive review and recommend them to a few friends when they praise your sharp look.

Your sales team should personally connect with your prospects in the marketing funnel to gather information on their problem area, which could help convert them into sales and return customers. A happy customer always leaves a positive review that you could leverage to gain credibility and acquire new customers. People believe reviews because a third party gives them. Just imagine, if 1000 people buy your product and only 50% of them leave positive 5-star reviews, that's 500 reviews, my friend. If someone notices 500 people praising a product, they are more likely to buy it – train your sales team to ask for feedback after every delivery.

Salespeople hold the key to your success. They establish connections with your customers and form the foundation of your company's reputation. It is recommended to have a reward structure for your sales team when converting a prospect into customer and then increasing a customer's retention rate; most companies offer the reward in the form of commission. It known that people seldom change their product choice one finding the best fit for them. Have you gone to Walmart or any mall to get toothpaste? There are dozens of options available, yet you seem to pick the one you've been using for months, if not years. Therefore, it is in your company's best interest to provide a reward structure for your sales team.

A fantastic way to grow a positive relationship with your customers is by scheduling a follow-up call or email once they have used your company's services. The follow-up can also be used as an opportunity to receive a positive review. It is advised to send an appreciation email thanking them for their business with a link to review your business in the email. Furthermore, your team can schedule a follow-up call after a few days or weeks to ensure they are pleased with their purchase. Construct a set of questions your team can follow during the call, such as; inquiring if the customer is satisfied with your company's services and if their problem is solved?

If they are satisfied, your team should ask if they wouldn't mind leaving a positive review after the call. The review process needs to be effortless for your client. A great way to make the process effortless is to ensure your team sends an email to your customer straight after the call with a direct link to your review page asking them to review their experience.

You can even offer a gift in return for a review, such as a 5% discount on their next purchase. For instance, suppose the customer experiences any issues or has any complaints; in that case, they can inform your team, and your team must resolve their queries. Have a system in place for when these issues arise, so your team knows how to handle them. Also, track the negative feedback; remember that all feedback is positive if used as an opportunity for growth, better your services, and solve problems to avoid negative reviews in the future. It is more cost-efficient to retain an existing client than to acquire a new one. Never underestimate the power of sales. Train your sales team to produce effective results every time. As you know by now, make it a process; call it the review process. You're welcome!

Sales Strategy

An effective plan to sell your products and services to increase your revenue is called a sales strategy. It is a tried and tested plan to gain desired results. Your master product is nothing if there are no people to buy it. Therefore, having a sales strategy in place is crucial from day one. It enhances the product awareness and chances to sell. There are two types of sales strategies – inbound and outbound.

The inbound sales strategy involves using various platforms like social media, blogs, email marketing, SEO, events, websites etc., to build awareness about your business, educate them, and encourage them to make a purchase and your sales team close the sale as discussed previously. You've defined your target audience's pain point, and you know they are looking for the solutions your company offers. In the midst, you offer them the ray of hope that will fix everything. As a result, they will buy your product.

The outbound strategy involves your sales team contacting the prospect directly to make them aware of your business. Unfortunately, in this strategy, your target audience isn't aware of your business. Therefore, your sales team needs to do a little more work than previously stated. First, they have to commit to cold calling, emailing, etc., to get their attention. This method is challenging because the prospect has never heard of your company and most people nowadays hate cold calls; I know I do for sure. However, if your team can gain their interest, they should proceed with the normal inbound marketing and selling strategy.

The key to sales success is obtaining cash flow and profits. You have no business if you can't encourage people to pay you for your product/service. For some people, converting a prospect into a sale is as hard as moving a mountain, while for others, it's a walk in the park. Why? Well, it's not that they are built differently, but because they have different qualities.

Success comes after you've taught your sales team how to master the 3As – Attitude, Activity, and Ability.

The attitude I referred to above isn't limited to the skills and confidence of your salesperson, but rather believing in the product, feeling proud and excited about selling it, and honestly believing in the service you offer. Is your sales team able to make your customers feel as enthusiastic about the product or service as they are? If the answer is NO, then getting substantial sales is going to be a sizable challenge. Therefore, implement enough training for your sales team to ensure they fully understand your company's services, have team-building exercises in place to make them excited and passionate, and ensure that they love your company as much as you do so that their passion seeks through into their sales.

Activity is about doing the work by using the marketing strategies, pulling people into the funnel, and then educating them into buying the product or service. If your team isn't active enough to get more leads, there will be no revenue to survive upon. Therefore, to ensure a continuous flux of leads, create prospect and lead goal, which consists of the number of lead your marketing team should be generating and prospects you sales team should be communicating with per day, week, and year. All clients and customers should be kept in the loop with scheduled follow-up call for that extra effect. Most sma businesses rely only on a few marketing approaches - if any at all. For example, social media or email; however, if you could effectively help your team to use multiple approaches, the magnitude of sales and revenue generation will be on par with no other. Let each of your salespeople have a conversion rate of their own; it can be reflected in their KPIs. Reward the best and help the rest.

Teach your team to uncover the needs of a customer while they are engaging with them. There are two crucial elements to remember. The first is that buying is more of an emotional decision than a rational one. People buy with emotions and then justify them with logic. The emotion could be desire, pain, fear, etc. The second element is that people don't care about the features; they only care about how it can benefit them. When your team can successfully identify their emotions and provide them with appropriate benefits, their conversion rate will skyrocket.

A great salesperson asks questions. Your team should know how to strategically ask intelligent questions to make your customers willingly give away their emotional triggers. It is recommended to let your customers do 90% of the talking. Your team's job is to ask questions, listen to the answers, and analyze the situation. Don't let them think about the closure – make them stay in the moment and chat with the customers; they will sell more. Sales is a skill that can be developed. Nobody is naturally phenomenal in sales. If your team needs training and polishing, embrace that they are willing to learn. Give them the guidance and resources to master their skills. They will love it, and when they be in a good mood, they will keep your customers happy. Hurry, move out! A giant wave of revenue is coming your way!

THE PSYCHOLOGY OF BUYING

I mentioned earlier that buying is an emotional decision. This section will teach you about the psychology of buying and how the mind works during a purchase. Antonio Damasio, a neuroscience professor, proved the concept of brains' response to emotions over rational thinking in 1994. This revolutionary study changed the neuroscience and marketing industry forever. He studied that impaired or damaged brains that lacked any emotional aspect struggled to make a decision. Our brain is divided into the core called the limbic brain, and the outer brain also referred to as the neocortex brain.

The limbic brain has two parts. One is responsible for survival instincts like breathing, hunger, and danger alerts while the other handles our emotions and feelings. The neocortex brain is fully responsible for logic, intelligence, communication, and decision making. It is also used to control our emotions. In theory, every outer stimulus should first go our outer brain, where it will rationalize it, and then move to the core limbic brain, which will trigger emotional responses. However, since the outer brain is not fully developed, it sometimes isn't capable of handling the outer stimulus, which is an outside source of feelings like anger, fear, etc. So instead, the signal goes directly to the core, where it automatically triggers our emotions. Now you know why you jump 10 feet after seeing a spider closer to you.

So, why am I telling you this? As a business owner, this is the system you need to be aware of, so that you can instantly communicate to the core limbic brain of your customers to regulate an emotional impulse purchase. When a person is emotionally attached to anything, they are more likely to flow at the moment. You cannot only use logic to justify why they should invest in your company. You need the limbic brain. Various motivations can drive people's emotions, such as love, greed, pride, fear, etc. These are the emotions you need to target if you are looking to sell a premium product. For example, if you're selling a high-end luxury car, you can tell them that "they have the money and this is how they should enjoy their money, buy that car" or "people will see you differently; all your social insecurities will be over."

Conversely, suppose you want to appeal to the general public. In that case, you need to tap into other motivations like competition, a sense of belonging, gratification, being the first, saving time, etc. Your team must communicate with customers and ask them a series of questions to know in which segment their emotions lie in and then tap into those emotions to help them make a purchase decision. Your team can do it by having a command of their language and showing social proof, using stories and pictures to engage, or by demonstrating empathy.

Knowing this, how many ideas of capitalizing on the marketplace emerged within your mind? I know you can hardly wait to imply those ideas and gain tremendous results. I wish you the best of luck with your business growth and would love to hear your success story. Please go to amazon and provide positive feedback for this book. It will help others to make their decision and get this book. You are helping the next person to gain the same knowledge that you just gained. While you're a it, refer this book to your friends, family members, and colleagues. See what I did there? I used the same psychology taught you about making an emotional connection to encourag people to do what you want - just walking my talk.

Don't forget to download the free workbook I promised yo earlier. For your convenience, I've given you two ways to get th workbook:

Scaling Up Simplified

SCAN THE CODE NOW

1. Here is the QR code for you. Take out your phone and scan it properly. After that, follow the same process as mentioned in the second step. You will soon have your own workbook.

2. You can click on the following link >>SCALING UP SIMPLIFIED WORKBOOK<< then, add your name and email address; and a conformational email will be sent to that specific address. Once you click the "confirm my subscription" button in the email; you will receive the free workbook within 10 minutes. Keep tabs on your inbox and "promotion folder", I might surprise you with the email anywhere, let's see!

We are now moving towards conclusion, which summarizes all the key lessons you learned in this fantastic book. It will brush up your memory and provide specific tasks to fulfill your goals and achieve your dreams. Are you ready?

KEY TAKEAWAYS

"Business is a long-term game of MAP – Mindset, Attitude and Persistence. In order to win, you must be all in."

– Shannon Teague

I t was a fantastic journey with you. I enjoyed it a lot, and I know that you did too. The question is, how much did you like it? Show your numbers on the Amazon review page. Is it a 5-star book or a 4.9-star book? We are on the final crossroad together, and it will be worth it for you. This part will summarize all the key lessons explained in this book to help you succeed in your business. With that said, let's begin with the first chapter.

Chapter 1:

It is designed to help you attain the mindset of a winner. No one can become successful unless they have the mindset to make it happen. Winning is 80% psychology and 20% skills. There is nothing you can't achieve if you put your heart and soul into it. You are enough; you have it in you – believe that you're destined for greatness. Difficult roads often lead to some beautiful destinations, and I want this road to end with you having the final laugh. Shifting perception is only impactful when you keep your emotions in check and do things beneficial to you and your business. Most people allow their feelings and emotions to overpower them. That result has consequences – be in control, explore your opportunities, and don't let any negative beliefs hold you back.

Chapter 2:

Habit is the result of repetition. You become what you repeatedly do. For example, our brain strives to save energy, and the way it does it is by installing small programs into our brain that trigger our movement without wasting too much energy. So, to install any habit in your brain, all you have to do is commit to it at a particular time every day for more than 30 days. Successful people become so by bringing positive growth-oriented habits into their life that makes them smarter, faster, and more prosperous. Their habits include journaling, exercise opposing negativity, learning daily, and networking with high-profile individuals. Use the cue, routine, and reward structure to internalize a habit.

Prepare a default diary and structure it well for yourself t help you allocate your time better and be more productive. D you remember the 80/20 rule? 80% of your business growt comes from 20% of your clients and processes. Find that 20 and amplify. Build processes and systems so that you work O your business rather than IN your business.

Chapter 3:

This chapter emphasizes goal setting. Goals begin with visualization, and the power to see what you can have, is on par with no other. The more you see it, the closer you can get to it. The simple process to visualize includes aiming the outcome, imagining it in a detailed manner, and repeating this exercise daily. One of the most potent ways to do it is by the vision board. You can have your dream in front of you and see it every day. Next, you need to set smart goals to reach your ultimate vision. S.M.A.R.T. means Specific, Measurable, Achievable, Relevant, and Time-bound.

Once you know your ultimate vision, you can break it down to yearly, quarterly, monthly, weekly, and even daily goals. I call them checkpoints. Organize your days and build a success plan for yourself and your business.

Chapter 4:

Look at all great businesses; they are on top because of their culture and values. Good culture makes people stick with you for a long time, while a negative culture repels them to seek another offer. A vision statement is a direct sentence that relates where the company aspires to be in the upcoming years, and without it, you as a leader and everyone who follows you will have no sense of direction. Write down your vision statement and look at it every day. It should unite everyone, inspire them, and have a single purpose. A mission statement is a literal definition, stating what a brand or company is setting out to accomplish—having strong core values drive the business forward and protect it internally and externally.

Company culture is an integral part of your business, and it impacts most of the organization's attributes, from recruiting top performers to enhancing their overall work satisfaction. Employees feel great and perform at their highest level when provided with a positive, healthy, and growth environment. Use wellness, provide purpose, create goals, elevate positivity, and the other five tips stated in the book to build a positive company culture.

Chapter 5:

Building a successful business requires recruiting people who fi your profile and match your company's culture and values. The critical thing to remember about hiring is that we are hirin; team members that will work IN our business so that we ca work ON our business; your end goal is to remove yourself fror the company. Set up an organizational chart from day on specifying every role and its duties. This chart will have all th positions required in your business like a manager, CFO, CE(technician, marketer, etc. To make this process easier, yo should take yourself three years into the future and imagir where you see your company. What are the functions require for you, and how will it operate?

The 5 key functions include finance, sales and marketing, customer support and service, admin management, and operations. Hire people who align with your company's culture by advertising a clear and attractive job description. Use the video strategy to filter out applicants and save time. Make your most potential candidates take on the talent dynamics profile test to define their personality type. Finally, create an effective recruitment process by following the 15-step method explained in the book – ask strategic questions in every step of the recruitment process to refine your candidates. Have a career page on your website displaying your company's culture, vision, values, history, and apply button.

Utilize the power of KPIs to measure the performance of your team. First, let your recruits have a probation period to test their strengths and weaknesses and make them undergo induction training. Then, take scheduled meetings with your staff to check their progress and discuss the upcoming events.

Chapter 6:

This chapter explains how you can run a successful business without constant involvement by using the systems and processes. It provides efficiency, accuracy and saves time by eliminating your continuous input. Your business needs customer assimilation, interfacing, retraction, budgeting, tax reduction, and other 15 processes illustrated in this chapter to make your business run smoothly. A simple way to be more productive, enhance creativity, and be organized is to use a checklist that has all your tasks written in it, and once you finish them, check it off.

Despite the implication of robust systems and processes, you will still be the leader who will drive your business forward. Leadership is the crucial component of running a business. You need someone to manage your systems and staff, inspire them, and track their progress. If you can't do it yourself, hire someone to do it for you. That is how you delegate the tasks you're not good at to someone who is an expert - do what you do the best. Use the following five steps to delegate like a pro:

- **Step 1:** Decide what to delegate
- **Step 2:** Clarify the expectations and processes
- **Step 3:** Empower your staff
- **Step 4:** Learn to let go
- **Step 5:** Invest your time and reap greater rewards

If you're still worried about the delegation process, use CRM software to delegate efficiently and ensure higher quality. Some of the best software available out there are:

- **Monday.com** (we partnered with them for you. Use the QR code in chapter 6.)

- **Trello**

Chapter 7:

Cash is the king. Finance is an essential element of your business. No business can survive, let alone scale, without cash flow. Establish a healthy financial system and process in your business. It involves having a business bank account, paying yourself a salary, keeping your manufacturing costs and all other costs low, exploring your options, and doing whatever you can to have extra cash in your business account. Learn the difference between good debt and bad debt – one takes you closer to your dream, while the other ruins it. Go through the "accounting basics" section to understand the foundational aspect of your business so that you don't commit the same mistake I did and waste capital.

If you don't have one, create a balance sheet and an income statement for your business using the steps provided in the chapter. Hire an accountant or a bookkeeper and manage them well so that they can proffer you with legal advice, save you money, and guide you in decision-making. Find the best accountant who understands you and your business, someone who fits in your culture and shares your values. Use accounting software to be on the same page as your accountant, have an analytical report with you every time, and to have a meaningful conversation with your accountant. Finally, develop a financial procedure using the steps explained in this chapter.

Chapter 8:

Business growth is the result of strategic marketing. If you successfully implement marketing, it will educate your customers, keep them engaged, create a strong reputation about your company in their minds, and smartly sell to them; your business will most likely make wonders. Build a brand bible illustrating all the business needs such as color palettes, fonts, images, logo, culture, values, purpose, vision, etc. Conduct research to decide a unique selling proposition for your product or service that will make you stand out from the crowd – use the steps in the book to create a USP for your product.

The only way to scale a business is by adding value. The value gained by the customer from your product or service is called a value proposition. It involves fulfilling the promise you made to your customer. So, go ahead and create an irresistible value proposition for your product that will amaze your customers and grow your business. For that to work, you need marketing strategy to successfully position your product and market it in front of your potential customers. Use the AIDA model to build a funnel to draw people in and convert them into customers. Explore approaches such as content, email, and social media marketing, SEO, public relations, advertising, and integrity. The 7-step marketing strategy builder includes the following:

1. Creating a marketing plan
2. Creating a customer's image
3. Understanding your goals
4. Using effective tools
5. Scrutinizing existing resources
6. Inspecting and planning
7. Taking massive action and achieving your goals

Lead generation is the process of finding people who are interested in your product and bringing them into your funnel. There are 3.96 billion people active on social media platforms, and you can use these platforms to gain leads. Next, become a master deliverer by delivering the value your business promises and excelling in each of the following areas: supply, quality, ease of purchase, and service. Finally, train your staff to connect with your customers and turn them into raving fans using the 8-step process explained in the chapter.

Take care of your sales team because they will generate revenue for you by taking care of your customers – they hold the key to your business success. One of the great ways for your team to build a positive connection with your customers is to set up a follow-up call to resolve their queries and gain feedback.

Next, you need to create a sales strategy, whether inbound, outbound, or a combination of two.

Your sales team needs to master the 3As – Attitude, Activity, and Ability to gain success. The psychology of buying refers to the underdeveloped outer brain rather than the core brain, which handles our emotions. Therefore, when you use powerful triggers, the information skips the external brain and goes directly into the limbic brain, causing people to make an emotional decision. As a business owner, your job is to train your team to hit their customers' core by using emotional triggers (fear, greed, love, pride, competition, gratification, etc.) to help them make a purchase.

There you have it, the book you've been waiting for, and it's finally yours to harness all the knowledge within. I hope you've enjoyed this book. I'll know how much you've enjoyed it; do you wonder how? I can see the number of stars and the feedback you give on Amazon. I am looking forward to reading your feedback and business-changing experiences. Next time, see you with unique and entertaining solution to a frustrating business problem – stick around!

Until then,
Keep leading, keep building, and keep making an impact!

Shannon Teague

****

RESOURCES

llen, R. (2017, January 17). *Evergreen marketing quotes to inspire your 2017 strategy*. Smart Insights.
https://www.smartinsights.com/digital-marketing-strategy/marketing-quotes-strategy/

> Marketing strategy is where we play and how we win in the market. Tactics are how we can deliver on the strategy and execute for success.

nabelle Walsch. (n.d.). *Uncategorized* |. Retrieved August 20, 2021, from
https://hackstohappy.com/category/uncategorized/

> *When you go from a fixed mindset to a growth mindset, a new world of possibilities opens up.*

st Accounting Quotes images to share and download at QuotesLyfe. (n.d.). Quoteslyfe.
trieved August 20, 2021, from https://www.quoteslyfe.com/category/accounting-quotes

> Don't ever let your business get ahead of the financial side of your business. Accounting, accounting, accounting. Know your numbers.

iss, P. (n.d.). *25 processes every business needs* | *Process Bliss*. Process Bliss. Retrieved August 20, 2021,
from https://processbliss.com/business-processes/

ian Tracy Quote: âThe checklist is one of the most high powered productivity tool ever discovered.â. (n.d.).
Quote Fancy. Retrieved August 20, 2021, from https://quotefancy.com/quote/777900/Brian-Tracy-The-checklist-is-one-of-the-most-high-powered-productivity-tool-ever

> The checklist is one of the most high powered productivity tool ever discovered.

ce Lee Quote*. (n.d.). A-Z Quotes. Retrieved August 20, 2021, from
https://www.azquotes.com/quote/171368

> I fear not the man who has practiced 10,000 kicks once, but I fear the man who has practiced one kick 10,000 times.

lker, T., McCullough, A., Bunce, D., McCullough, A., Chalker, T., McCullough, A., Bunce, D., &
McCullough, A. (n.d.). *The Power of Vision Boards*. The Bruns. Retrieved August 20, 2021, from
https://www.thebruns.ca/articles/the-power-of-vision-boards

> Your brain will work tirelessly to achieve the statements you give your subconscious mind. And when those statements are the affirmations and images of your goals, you are destined to achieve them.

, A. P. T. |. (2021, March 21). *5 Benefits of Developing the Right Habits*. Productive and Free.
https://www.productiveandfree.com/blog/benefits-of-habits

> Your net worth to the world is usually determined by what remains after your bad habits are subtracted from your good ones.
> You'll never change your life until you change something you do daily. The secret of your success is found in your daily routine.

ey Mackay Quote*. (n.d.). A-Z Quotes. Retrieved August 20, 2021, from
https://www.azquotes.com/quote/183041

> Delegating doesn't mean passing off work you don't enjoy, but letting your employees stretch their skills and judgment.

does CRM help you delegate better?* (n.d.). International. Retrieved August 20, 2021, from
https://www.teamleader.eu/blog/how-crm-helps-you-delegate-better

20, January 9). *20 Inspirational Quotes Relating to a Healthy Mindset*. Jane Taylor | Transition Coach |
Engagement Coach | Wellbeing Coaching | Mindful Self-Compassion Coaching | Gold Coast |
Mindfulness Teacher. https://www.habitsforwellbeing.com/inspirational-quotes-relating-to-a-healthy-mindset/

> *You have power over your mind - not outside events. Realize this, and you will find strength.*

John Spence Quote: âMy definition of success: When your core values and self-concept are in harmony with your daily actions and behaviors.â. (n.d.). Quote Fancy. Retrieved August 20, 2021, from https://quotefancy.com/quote/1698035/John-Spence-My-definition-of-success-When-your-core-values-and-self-concept-are-in

> My definition of success: When your core values and self-concept are in harmony with your daily actions and behaviors.

Mussetter, N. (2018, October 23). *Default Diary - A guide to blocking and rocking your day!* Nacre. https://www.nacre.com.au/default-diary

> Each week, I have Management Monday, a day where I focus mostly on business development tasks. Ideas and tasks for business development obviously arise throughout the week, but because I know I've got time allotted for those already, I don't have to drop what I'm doing to brainstorm an idea. I just note the task or idea down and tackle it when the day comes around. Some blocks may be allotted weekly, and some fortnightly, depending on how much time they need in a given month.

> I'll usually spend a day each month on Marketing Magic. This is perfect for me as it breaks marketing down into manageable chunks that I know I can focus on for a day then put aside; knowing that they'll be added to the coming month.

> Twice a month I've also set aside 90-minute blocks for financial matters. So, if invoicing is a task that keeps slipping on your list then you'll want to try a default diary for financial matters for sure.

Press, Discover. (2021). *Power of Habit: Rewire Your Brain to Build Better Habits and Unlock Your Full Potential.* GTM Press LLC.

Quote, B. (2020, June 17). *35 Possibility quotes that will make you think positively.* Be Inspired from Famous Quotes | Bliss Quote. https://www.blissquote.com/2020/06/possibility-quotes.html

> When you have no fear, the possibilities are endless.

Quotes about delegation in business Dave ramsey quote âdelegation requires the willingness to pay for. (n.d.). Dog Training Obedience School. Retrieved August 20, 2021, from https://dogtrainingobedienceschool.com/quotes-about-delegation-in-business/7545168_dave-ramsey-quote-delegation-requires-the-willingness-to-pay-for.html

> Delegation requires the willingness to pay for the short-term failures, in order to gain long term competency.

Quotes About Making Things Complicated. QuotesGram. (n.d.). Quotes Gram. Retrieved August 20, 2021, from https://quotesgram.com/quotes-about-making-things-complicated/

> Any intelligent fool can make things bigger, more complex, and more violent. It takes touch of genius and a lot of courage to move in the opposite direction.

Recruitee. (2020, December 12). *How a careers page helps your employer brand.* https://blog.recruitee.com/careers-page/

Roy, B. D. (2021, August 17). *100 Thought-Provoking Company Culture Quotes.* Nurture an Engaged and Satisfied Workforce | Vantage Circle HR Blog. https://blog.vantagecircle.com/company-culture-quotes/

> Corporate culture matters. How management chooses to treat its people impacts everything for better or for worse.

> Company culture is the backbone of any successful organization.

> You can have all the right strategies in the world; if you don't have the right culture, you're dead.

> There's no magic formula for great company culture. The key is just to treat your staff how you would like to be treated.

Say, J. (2020, June 20). *104 Darren Hardy Quotes (THE COMPOUND EFFECT).* Gracious Quotes. https://graciousquotes.com/darren-hardy/

Tracking my progress and missteps is one of the reasons I've accumulated the success I have.

'ay, J. (2021, January 5). *49 Motivational Quotes for Startups (SUCCESS)*. Gracious Quotes. https://graciousquotes.com/startups/

Spend time upfront to invest in systems and processes to make long-term growth sustainable.

MART Goals: – How to Make Your Goals Achievable. (n.d.). Mind Tools. Retrieved August 20, 2021, from https://www.mindtools.com/pages/article/smart-goals.htm

Your goal should be clear and specific, otherwise, you won't be able to focus your efforts or feel truly motivated to achieve it. When drafting your goal, try to answer the five "W" questions:

What do I want to accomplish?

Why is this goal important?

Who is involved?

Where is it located?

Which resources or limits are involved?

aff, S. (2018, July 31). *17 Motivational Quotes to Inspire Successful Habits*. SUCCESS. https://www.success.com/17-motivational-quotes-to-inspire-successful-habits/

Depending on what they are, our habits will either make us or break us. We become what we repeatedly do.

Good habits are worth being fanatical about.

eatt, L. (2021, March 3). *18 Motivational Quotes About Successful Goal Setting*. SUCCESS. https://www.success.com/18-motivational-quotes-about-successful-goal-setting/

If you want to be happy, set a goal that commands your thoughts, liberates your energy, and inspires your hopes.

All who have accomplished great things have had a great aim have fixed their gaze on a goal which was high, one which sometimes seemed impossible.

Our goals can only be reached through a vehicle of a plan, in which we must fervently believe, and upon which we must vigorously act. There is no other route to success.

Success is the progressive realization of a worthy goal or ideal.

nt Dynamics Profile Test | Welcome. (n.d.). Talent Dynamics Profile Test. Retrieved August 20, 2021, from https://www.tdprofiletest.com/home/#

Talent Dynamics is different in that it provides an intuitive structure, practical strategies, modern role models, and a link back to the roots of profiling 5,000 years ago.

ve Agency. (2020, December 21). *Why is having a company vision so important for business?* Thrive Internet Marketing Agency. https://thriveagency.com/news/business-vision/

You've got to give yourself the freedom to dream – to use your imagination to see and feel what does not yet exist. A vision is not the same as goals or objectives; those come from the head. A vision comes from the heart.

14 LIMITED PERSPECTIVE QUOTES. (n.d.). A-Z Quotes. Retrieved August 20, 2021, from https://www.azquotes.com/quotes/topics/limited-perspective.html

Your perspective is always limited by how much you know. Expand your knowledge and you will transform your mind.

Don't be trapped by dogma — which is living with the results of other people's thinking.

25 ACCOUNTING QUOTES (of 221). (n.d.). A-Z Quotes. Retrieved August 20, 2021, from https://www.azquotes.com/quotes/topics/accounting.html

The word accounting comes from the word accountability. If you are going to be rich, you need to be accountable for your money.

accounting is the language of business.

TOP 25 QUOTES BY FRED WILSON (of 60). (n.d.). A-Z Quotes. Retrieved August 20, 2021, from
https://www.azquotes.com/author/15775-Fred_Wilson

> Investing in management means building communication systems, business processes, feedback, and routines that let you scale the business and team as efficiently as possible.

Understanding Key Performance Indicators (KPIs). (n.d.). Investopedia. Retrieved August 20, 2021, from
https://www.investopedia.com/terms/k/kpi.asp

Why Mission Statements Matter. (n.d.). Investopedia. Retrieved August 20, 2021, from
https://www.investopedia.com/terms/m/missionstatement.asp

> a company's mission statement defines its culture, values, ethics, fundamental goals, and agenda. In addition to that, it defines how each of these applies to the company's stakeholders — like its employees, distributors, suppliers, shareholders, and the community at large. Use this statement to align their goals with that of the company. The statement reveals what the company does, how it does it, and why it does it

Y. (2021a, May 1). *60 Consistency Quotes To Keep You Going Smoothly (2021)*. YourFates.
https://www.yourfates.com/consistency-quotes/

> Being persistent may lead you to the door but is the key that unlocks it.

Y. (2021b, August 3). *55 Motivational Success Quotes to Achieve Your Kind of Success (2021)*. YourFates.
https://www.yourfates.com/success-quotes/

> Success is the sum of small efforts, repeated day-in, and day-out.
> Life is not about finding yourself. Life is about creating yourself.

Yalım, D. (2021, April 3). *125+ EXCLUSIVE Vision Quotes to See Unique Magic*. BayArt.
https://bayart.org/vision-quotes/

> Vision is the art of seeing what is invisible to others.

Zojceska, A. (2020, April 3). *Top 10 Inspirational HR and Recruiting Quotes*. Blog.
https://www.talentlyft.com/en/blog/article/195/top-10-inspirational-hr-and-recruiting-quotes

> Nothing we do is more important than hiring and developing people. At the end of the day, you bet on people, not on strategies.

> The competition to hire the best will increase in the years ahead. Companies that give extra flexibility to their employees will have the edge in this area.

Campbell, K. (2018, January 3). *Your Primer to the Psychology of Marketing: The Science of Emotional Buy and What Marketers Can Do About It*. The BigCommerce Blog.
https://www.bigcommerce.co.uk/blog/marketing-psychology/#undefined

Carmicheal, K. (2021, February 4). *The Step-by-Step Guide to Creating a Complete Marketing Strategy in 2021*. Hubspot. https://blog.hubspot.com/marketing/marketing-strategy

Cousins, C. (2013, May 13). *How to Build a Brand Bible & Visual Style Guide*. Design Shack.
https://designshack.net/articles/graphics/how-to-build-a-brand-bible-visual-style-guide/

Defining Your Expectations For Delivery Mastery. (n.d.). Online Business Coach. Retrieved August 22, 202
from https://www.onlinebusinesscoach.com/articles-database/defining-your-expectations-for-delive
mastery

Developing your USP: A step-by-step guide. (n.d.). Marketing Donut. Retrieved August 22, 2021, from
https://www.marketingdonut.co.uk/marketing-strategy/branding/developing-your-usp-a-step-by-ste
guide

Munson, H. (2017, January 30). *How to Make a Marketing Plan for Your Small Business*. Bluehost Blog.
https://www.bluehost.com/blog/how-to-make-a-marketing-plan/

Sales Strategy - The Complete Guide (With Free Template!). (n.d.). Freshworks. Retrieved August 22, 202
from https://www.freshworks.com/crm/sales/sales-strategy/

Unique selling point. (n.d.). Optimizely. Retrieved August 22, 2021, from
https://www.optimizely.com/optimization-glossary/unique-selling-point/

Value Proposition. (n.d.). Optimizely. Retrieved August 22, 2021, from
    https://www.optimizely.com/optimization-glossary/value-proposition/

www.vernard.net. (2019, February 7). *Lead Generation*. ActionCOACH.
    https://www.actioncoach.com/blog/lead-generation/

Roy, B. D. (2021, May 23). *7 Ways to Build a Strong Company Culture*. Nurture an Engaged and Satisfied
    Workforce | Vantage Circle HR Blog. https://blog.vantagecircle.com/build-strong-company-culture/

What is a KPI? Definition, Best-Practices, and Examples. (n.d.). Klipfolio.Com. Retrieved September 13, 2021,
    from https://www.klipfolio.com/resources/articles/what-is-a-key-performance-
    indicator#SMARTERKPI

Printed in Great Britain
by Amazon

75064161R00151